THE PEAK DISTRICT COMPANION

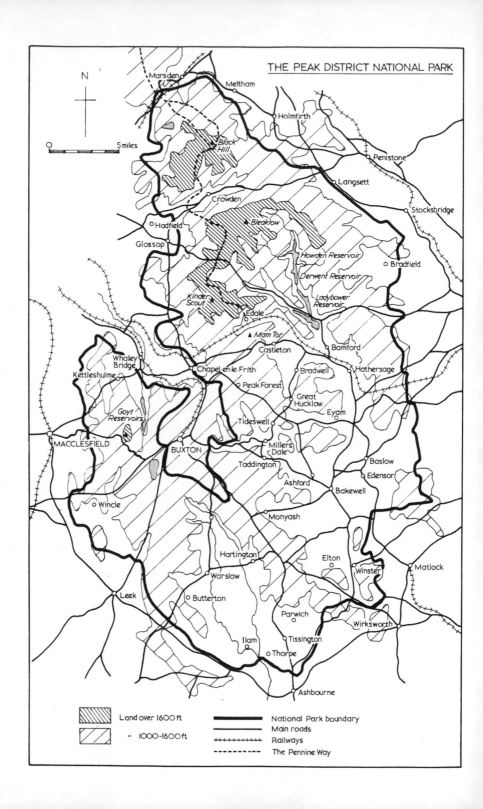

THE PEAK DISTRICT NATIONAL PARK

N

5 miles

Marsden
Meltham
Holmfirth
Black
Hill
Penistone
Langsett
Crowden
Stocksbridge
Hadfield
Bleaklow
Glossop
Howden Reservoir
Bradfield
Derwent Reservoir
Kinder
Scout
Ladybower
Reservoir
Edale
Mam Tor
Bamford
Castleton
Bradwell
Hathersage
Whaley
Bridge
Chapel-en-le-Frith
Kettleshulme
Peak Forest
Great
Hucklow
Eyam
Goyt
Reservoirs
Tideswell
MACCLESFIELD
Millers
Dale
Baslow
BUXTON
Edensor
Taddington
Ashford
Bakewell
Wincle
Monyash
Hartington
Elton
Winster
Matlock
Warslow
Leek
Butterton
Parwich
Wirksworth
Ilam
Tissington
Thorpe
Ashbourne

Land over 1600 ft   National Park boundary
                           Main roads
" 1000-1600 ft   Railways
                           The Pennine Way

THE
PEAK DISTRICT
COMPANION

A Walker's Guide
to its Fells, Dales and History

REX BELLAMY

Photographs by Don Bellamy

DAVID & CHARLES
Newton Abbot   London   North Pomfret (Vt)

British Library Cataloguing in Publication Data

Bellamy, Rex
   The Peak District Companion
   1. Peak District, Eng.—Description and
   travel—Guidebooks
   I. Title
   914.25′11′04857   DA670.D43

ISBN 0 7153 8140 7

Library of Congress Catalog Card Number 80–70294

Filmset in Monophoto Plantin by
Latimer Trend & Company Ltd, Plymouth
and printed in Great Britain by
Redwood Burn Ltd, Trowbridge & Esher
for David & Charles (Publishers) Limited
Brunel House   Newton Abbot   Devon

Published in the United States of America
by David & Charles Inc
North Pomfret   Vermont 05053   USA

Contents

Introduction

The Peak District is neither. It contains hardly anything that corresponds with the connotations of the word 'peak' and it lacks the corporate identity associated with the word 'district'. True, it has a great deal of wild country around the 2,000ft mark but most of this has the contours and consistency of a half-used brown loaf stuck on its end and left out in the rain (to talk of a 'peat' district would be to show a readier grasp of the facts of life). The few bumps on the relevant section of the earth's crust that do approach the shape of peaks are on a lower level than the flat wasteland of Kinder Scout and Bleaklow. The situation is further confused by the fact that we are discussing a land in which high ground is often called a 'low'. The thing to remember is that 'péac' was old English for a 'hill' and that the people who settled between Manchester and Sheffield in the seventh century were called pecsaetans: hill-dwellers. Substituting 'hill' for 'peak' switches on the light of understanding.

Our 'district' is thinly populated and its small communities mostly have strongly independent identities and tend to be slightly exclusive about outsiders, even those living in the next village. On the whole these communities are too widely scattered for any corporate feeling to exist between them. It follows therefore that the Peak District as a whole has no social coherence. But there are two features that these hill-dwellers have in common. One is the fact that they are all stuck on the southern end of the Pennines, which means that geology, geography, climate and the rest have set them

7

apart from the flanking urban masses. The other is that in 1951 most of the Peak District – excluding only those areas in which development could not reasonably be controlled – was designated as Britain's first national park. Its claim to this pioneering priority was its location in the heart of England, with almost half of England's population within fifty miles. Even for Londoners the Peak District remains the nearest national park. This book, though, is concerned with the entire Peak District, not merely the 542 square miles within the park.

This southern limit of England's highland zone is also the point of transition between North and Midlands and a playground for both. It consists of two clearly defined types of scenery caused by different rocks. Hold a map of the Peak District vertical and the gritstone ranges are like a suspended horseshoe – with Kinder and Bleaklow taking the weight, as it were, and the two prongs falling down each side. This gritstone horseshoe is the barren, wild moorland of the Peak District. Within it is the relatively gentle, more productive limestone country. Not the least attractive feature of the Peak District is that it therefore offers walkers, climbers, and indeed all visitors two distinct types of scenery: gritstone moors and limestone dales.

The most obvious deficiency, of course, is the absence of the sea. But man has to some extent repaired nature's omission by creating the attractive lake scenery of Derwent Dale and the Goyt Valley. The introduction of such large stretches of water has also widened the scope of vegetation and animal and bird life – already of uncommon interest because of the transition from highland to lowland England and from gritstone country to limestone country. Water has always been of great importance to the Peak District. Many millions of years ago the entire area formed the bed of a clear, shallow, sheltered sea populated by the small change of marine life. The shell debris accumulated and hardened into limestone. Reefs were formed. Volcanic action lifted, contorted, and cracked the strata. And when that ancient sea receded, water continued to have a particularly interesting effect on the relatively porous limestone country, where such rivers as the Manifold, Hamps, and Lathkill have a curious knack of diving underground. The caverns, potholes, and other rocky peculiarities of the limestone region have their recreational counterparts in the majestic edges and bizarre outcrops of the gritstone moorland.

Prehistoric man, including the cave-dwellers, settled widely over the Peak District and left us exciting legacies. The Romans built roads and forts and had persistent problems with the fierce Brigantes. The Normans left their mark, too. The stories we have to tell concern people like Little John, Mary Queen of Scots, Charlotte Brontë and George Eliot, Florence Nightingale, and such revolutionary engineering and industrial figures as James Brindley and Richard Arkwright. In addition to such private traditions as well-dressing festivals, the Peak District has some enchanting old churches and mansions and more than its share of legends and ghost stories. I have examined the whole canvas with what has, I hope, been an objective affection – delighted when forced to conclude that what I wanted to believe was actually true, yet not shirking the need to debunk an appealing story when it was obviously nonsense.

It would be physically impossible to cover everything in this book within the span of one short holiday. But I hope you will select such items as especially interest you and then set out on a journey of exploration. If it takes you briefly into all the seven areas discussed, then you will improve your knowledge of the Peak District. In other words, grant at least one day's travelling to the subject matter of every chapter. If your means of transport often shifts from wheels to legs (as I hope it will) remember that the word 'park' is misleading. The Peak District is and always has been a home and a place of work for farmers and others, and most of the land is privately owned. That imposes on all of us a need to be considerate –

as we expect others to be if they visit us at home or at work. I could list a dozen and more items as a comprehensive country code. But it has been neatly summarised in the words:

Take nothing but photographs
Kill nothing but time
Leave nothing but footprints

For your basic factual information – and a wealth of it is available – consult the national park office at Bakewell or the information centres at Bakewell, Buxton, Castleton, or Edale (the southern extremity of the Pennine Way). When combining driving and walking, you may find the two-car trick useful if you are touring with friends. You want to walk from B to A? Both drive to A and park one car. Then all drive to B and park the other. You can now have a meandering walk through the country from B to A and collect each car in turn. The Peak District is superb walking country but its weather is unpredictable, particularly on the moorland wildernesses. You may set off lightly clad in bright sunshine and within half an hour – even less – find yourself soaked, shivering, and possibly lost in mist and rain. A fool is no hero.

Having advised you to read this book with care, to collect the brochures and leaflets from the information centres, to plan your journey and take sensible precautions, I have to take the edge from this avuncular advice by recognising the modern tendency to put the countryside under a microscope instead of simply enjoying it. The two approaches need not be mutually exclusive (even the confirmed bog-trotter will use a path if there is one handy). What I suggest is that you do your reading and thinking in advance, then head for the hills and dales and open your eyes and ears and mind and heart to all the impressions that crowd in on them. No need to rush about frantically, ticking off names on a list of locations. Take your time. Smell the flowers and listen to the music of the brooks and the birds. Look around and see what the Peak District has to say to you. And in the moments you set aside for rest and reflection, I hope you find this book the good companion it is meant to be.

Rex Bellamy
Bilberry Cottage, Seale

1
Dovedale and Supporting Cast

FROM CROMFORD AND WIRKSWORTH TO THE DOVE,
THE MANIFOLD AND MORRIDGE
See map pages 14–15

Prehistoric man came and went. So did the Romans, Bonnie Prince Charlie and George Eliot. So did the monastic granges, the lead-miners, the railways, and a lot of once-animated hamlets that are now no more than smudges on a vast landscape. All left faint imprints on the window that looks back into time. The analogy is perhaps most apt in the case of the railways. They have been converted into grooved trails where we can exercise body and mind: on foot or in the saddle (the saddle being attached to horse or bicycle according to habit and preference). It seemed a shame to let these man-made arteries decompose and become mere scars on the hills, so they were resurrected for recreational use. The rails and sleepers were torn up; the surface was improved where necessary; the derelict station buildings were demolished or repaired and adapted to their new function. Car parks, picnic sites, and toilets were installed – even water for the horses. Bicycles were made available for hire. Interesting digressions from the trails were signposted, information posts opened, and rangers and voluntary wardens appointed to shepherd the flock of tourists and round up any strays.

All this formalised channelling of rural exploration may seem horribly alien to those brought up to find their own way across the wild and often trackless moorlands of Kinder Scout and Bleaklow farther north. But most people are grateful for a little help along the way, rather than resenting it; and there are hordes of tourists who are strangers not only to the Peak District but to the countryside as a whole. Visitors are simply offered a trouble-free route across stimulating and attractive country in the heart of England. No cars. No motor cycles. No fumes. No noise. And as one ranger put it to me, the trails serve another useful purpose by widening the horizons – tempting people away from such congested spots as Dovedale.

The High Peak trail extends for more than seventeen miles along the old Cromford and High Peak Railway from Cromford to Dow Low, about four miles south-east of Buxton. Much of it is close to a faintly traceable Roman road. The Tissington trail, along thirteen miles of the former line between Ashbourne and Buxton, extends from Ashbourne to Parsley Hay (just off the A515, between Hartington and Monyash), where it joins the High Peak trail. A third trail, more loosely organised in the days before such things became fashionable, follows the meandering Waterhouses–Hulme End section of that brief venture, the Leek and Manifold Light Railway.

The trails are a pleasing memorial to the railway era. The CHPR was an engineering enterprise of remarkable boldness and ingenuity. Begun in 1825 and opened in 1830, a period when railway engineering was still primitive, the line extended from Cromford Wharf at 277ft to Whaley Bridge at 517ft. The tricky bit was in the middle, because the railway had to climb to 1,264ft and then come down again. The purpose was to transport heavy minerals between Cromford Canal at one end and Whaley Bridge (the Peak Forest Canal) at the other. The CHPR was so much a product of the canal age that the stations were called wharves. The nine inclines were the equivalent of locks. At first horses provided the locomotive power on the level stretches (steam engines came later) and the wagons were hauled up the inclines by stationary engines. One of these, in the octagonal engine house at Middleton Top, north-west of Wirksworth, has been restored to working order as a reminder of the way things were done

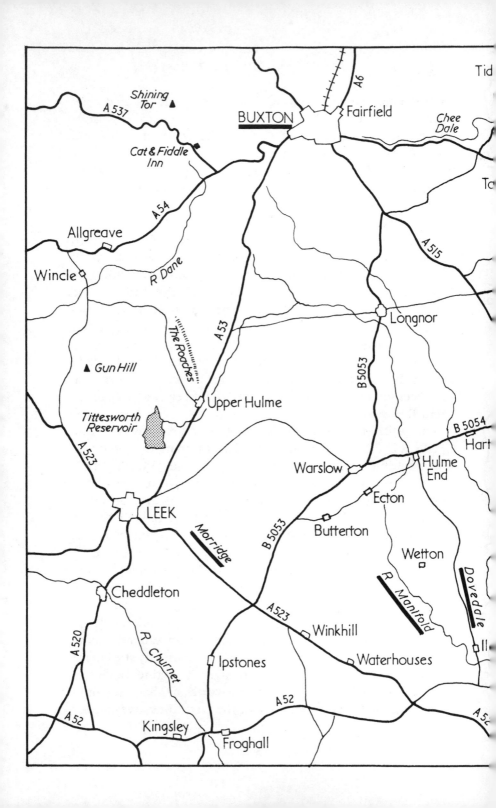

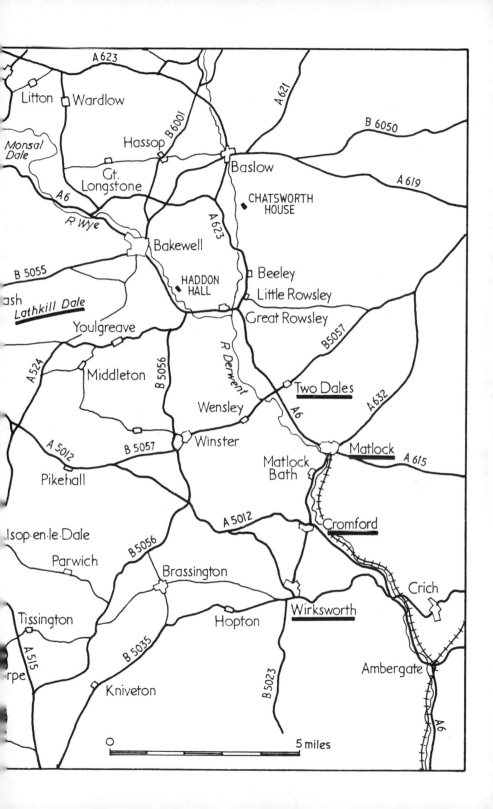

in 1830. Farther east is the Sheep Pasture Incline, which was equipped with a 'catch pit' after what must have been a spectacular accident in 1888, when two wagons broke free of restraint, hurtled downhill, and leapt from the track to clear both the canal and railway before plunging into a field. The 'catch pit' is still there, plus a few old railway buildings at High Peak Junction, where goods were transferred between the CHPR and the canal – later, between the CHPR and the main-line railway. The CHPR marked a transition from the age of canals and their contiguous tramways to that of the railways.

The CHPR stimulated the industrial exploitation of the Peak District's mineral resources but it could not resist the effects of changing patterns in industry and transport. Nor did passenger traffic provide the CHPR with an alternative financial cushion. This was never more than an appendage – a single carriage attached to a goods train – and it was stopped altogether after a fatal accident in 1877. Passenger travel cannot have been much fun anyway. There was never any certainty when trains would arrive or leave (partly because the harassed crews enjoyed relaxing in pubs along the way). The trains moved slowly because of the weight of the goods, the difficult terrain, and the occasional need to clear sheep off the line. And up the steeper inclines, often 1 in 8, passengers had to get out and walk.

The decline of track-side quarries inevitably hastened the decline of the CHPR. One section after another was closed, the last run being in 1967. But the memories are still fresh. There is still much evidence of the brave dreams of those engineers of 1825.

The Ashbourne–Buxton line, built for the London and North-Western Railway Company, was opened in 1899. It carried limestone, dairy produce, and passengers too, but was never much more than a branch line. Between 1954 and 1967 it was gradually phased out but, like the CHPR (closed the same year), it was adapted for a different function only four years later. The Tissington Trail, as it is known, cannot match its partner's historic significance in terms of engineering and industrial interest. On the other hand, though the Tissington Trail never strays far from the main road it is the more charming of the two trails in terms of scenery and nature study. Quarrying has not inflicted on it the same messy scars.

The stretch of the Leek and Manifold Light Railway relevant to this book was the eight miles of narrow-gauge track (2ft 6in) laid through a lovely, lonely valley from Waterhouses to the northern terminus at Hulme End. It operated for only thirty years, from 1904 to 1934. The idea was to carry farming produce from a string of high, isolated villages; to provide a limited passenger service; and to encourage a revival of lead-mining at Ecton Hill. In 1905 these hopes were nourished by the opening of a standard-gauge connecting line from Waterhouses to Leek. But the farming produce was gradually diverted to road transport, passengers soon lost their enthusiasm for slogging up and down the hills between the villages and the stations in the valley, and the mining revival never happened. So the line had no chance to prosper. Since 1937 it has been a track of a different kind. But in the mind's eye we can picture the lusty little engines chugging along the Hamps and Manifold valleys with their trains of primrose-painted carriages.

Not that I pictured it in youth. From Sheffield we used to set off by train, bus, or bicycle and head for the Hope Valley or the rugged wasteland north of it. The Wye valley was usually the limit of our concessions to the ladies and the gentler prettiness farther south. The car has made the Peak District smaller, easier to explore thoroughly. But it still seems odd for a bog-trotter to drive from the south into a relatively mild landscape dotted with A's, as if stuttering into the alphabet. Ashbourne, Ambergate, Alderwasley, Alport Hill . . .

Alport Hill, anyway, is a taste of the right stuff – diluted but

nevertheless authentic. This remote recurrence of the northern gritstone offers fine views from a height of 1,032ft,
and even has a pillar of rock on which climbers can flex their
muscles. Yes, Alport Hill will do for a start. Perhaps, having
done their chores farther north, the gods in charge of geological details had a sample to spare and chucked it south to
tempt the uninitiated in the right direction. There was a
settlement here in Roman days, when high society was more
prevalent than it is now. A mile and a half to the north-east
is Alderwasley, a pleasant hamlet that took its name from the
trees and commands impressive views across the thickly
wooded Derwent Valley. Shining Cliff Woods are a remnant
of an old hunting forest.

Down in the valley is Ambergate, a plain place flattered by
its setting. But Ambergate assumed some importance as a
junction of rivers, railways, and roads: and is consequently
well known as a side-entrance to the Peak District. The trip
north-west to Cromford should not be hurried. The valley
is beautiful and its narrow floor contains the unusual spectacle
of road, river, railway, and canal running along together in a
cosy proximity forced upon them by nature. This stretch of
the canal has been converted into what official jargon des-
cribes as 'an amenity waterway' (which means, among other
things, that it is the place to make for if you feel that life
would be incomplete without spending a little of it in a
horse-drawn barge). The Cromford Canal, which had the
Erewash Canal at one end and the CHPR at the other, was a
fifteen-mile section of a complicated transport network that
linked the Trent and Mersey. Opened in 1794, it was to
carry such heavy goods as coal, limestone, lead, and iron
products (from foundries near Ripley), and the less weighty
output of Cromford's cotton mills. Trade began to decline
after 1849 because a railway was built between Ambergate
and Manchester. But the canal was kept at work until 1938.

Cromford acquired its name from 'cruneford', which in
early English indicated 'a crooked ford'. It stood on a Roman

road, Hereward Street, that ran from Ashbourne to Wirks-worth, Matlock, and Chesterfield. A pig (block) of lead found on Cromford Moor dates from early in the second century. In Scarthin Nick, a limestone spur from which a slice was removed so that a road could be accommodated, a workman came across a cavity containing a human skeleton and more than sixty Roman coins. The Romans crossed the Derwent by a ford located in the same spot as the fifteenth-century bridge (since widened), which has pointed arches on one side and rounded arches on the other. Obviously the builder was either indecisive or mischievous. Imagine the scene, if you will, when a horseman was riding over that bridge, minding his own business, one day in June of 1697. Perhaps sensing Roman ghosts, the horse suddenly got excited and jumped the parapet into the river. Both waded out undamaged but thoughtful. The southern end of the bridge retains the remnants of a fifteenth-century chapel that was later secu-larised and used as a little house.

All this is interesting but not exceptional. The unique thing about Cromford is the revolutionary role this once-quiet hamlet was to play in industrial history. An introduc-tory episode occurred between 1629 and 1636. This was the construction of the Longhead Sough, designed by a Dutch engineer and drainage expert, Sir Cornelius Vermuyden, to divert water from the flooded Dove Gang lead mine – between Cromford and Wirksworth – into the Derwent. This sough (pronounced 'suff') was one of the earliest examples of the tunnels that were to permeate the mining area in the next 200 years. It was to serve its purpose until the deeper, more ambitious Cromford Sough was built between 1673 and 1682 (with an exit or 'tail' behind houses in the existing market place).

But the man who changed the face of Cromford was Richard Arkwright (1732–92). Born into a poor family at Preston, he became a barber's assistant and an itinerant wig-maker. He found out about dyeing hair and at hiring fairs he met spinners and weavers who aroused his interest in the textile business and its machinery. He invented a cotton-spinning machine that improved on James Hargreaves' 'Spinning Jenny'. But in Lancashire there was violent opposition to the introduction of machinery, so in 1768 Arkwright moved to Nottingham and built a mill using machinery of his own devising. It depended on horse power – and Arkwright thought water power was a better idea. He looked around, leased some land at Cromford, and found a like-minded partner in Jedediah Strutt (1726–97) of South Normanton, whose 'Derby Rib' machine took the hosiery industry into a new era.

The first English cotton-spinning mill powered by water was established at Cromford in 1771 and it was here, two years later, that calico was made for the first time. That mill was the basis for mechanisation and mass production in the textile business. It marked the beginning of the factory system and a social and industrial revolution in the North of England. On the lower floors of that first mill (some of which still stands, down the road from the Greyhound Hotel) there were no windows. The idea was to make access difficult and discourage the mob violence that might be provoked by the mechanised threat to family businesses: the 'cottage industry' based on hand-spinning, which inevitably did decline and eventually died.

A second mill was built downstream in 1777 and in the next seven years Arkwright, though pestered by lawsuits, had others built at Cressbrook and Bakewell, both on the Wye, and nearer home at Ashbourne, Wirksworth, and up the valley at Masson. This last mill, beside the Matlock road, entailed the construction of an unusual weir with an experimental, bulging design. Arkwright's aquatic arrangements also included the introduction of a small reservoir at Cromford and, inevitably, some of the initiative for the canal, though he died before the latter was opened.

By the time he was 50 (and still studying spelling and

grammar) Arkwright had demonstrated that he was socially as well as industrially enlightened. The fact that Cromford was spared 'trouble at t' mill' was doubtless due not only to the work he provided, but also to the way he transformed Cromford into the first industrial village of its kind. His workers, including the families of many miners, were given new houses such as those in North Street (1777), built with three storeys so that the upper floors could accommodate knitting machines for the manufacture of stockings. They were given a chapel (also in 1777), the Greyhound Hotel (1778), a school (1784), and a market (the first was in 1790). Still much as Arkwright left it, the village is gathered round the inn and the market place, downhill from the older hamlet. The whole area is a sturdy monument to a revolutionary period in English history. The only slightly incongruous feature, in terms of its purposes, is a restored eighteenth-century fishing pavilion that reminds us of Cromford's reputation for fly-fishing.

To reclothe hillsides bared by the lead-miners' insatiable need for wood, Arkwright also had trees planted – not in dozens, not in hundreds, but in thousands. His personal vanity took a form common enough in successful businessmen of his day. Knighted in 1786, he bought a manor, had the village of Willersley demolished, and began to build the pretentiously grand Willersley Castle – which vies with Chatsworth as the supposed model for the Pemberley of Jane Austen's *Pride and Prejudice*. He was never to live there. Still incomplete, the place was burnt down in 1791 and he died before it was rebuilt and finished. But his son lived there and the castle later became a Methodist guest-house. Arkwright died in Rock House (overlooking his Cromford mills), which was subsequently converted into flats. He was buried at the church then being erected – another of his initiatives – on the perimeter of the Willersley grounds. His son made sure that the church, like the castle, was completed. All the way to the grave, Arkwright was making things happen.

If you need a breather while digesting all that history, toddle up to the Black Rocks, just off the Wirksworth road. These impressive bumps have been popular with trippers since Victorian days. Climb them only if you really know your stuff. Otherwise, take a walk or simply enjoy the air and the scenery.

The town-hall clock at Wirksworth was the bequest of a Killer. There are three more (Killers, not clocks) in the local telephone directory. The place has been scarred by quarrying, and looks old and grey and too weary to bother dressing up for tourists. It need not detain you long. It detained me only because I wanted to check a few facts – and also yielded to a sudden craving for fish and chips, a craving satisfied in the presence of a jolly but unfortunate lady with a voice so insistently strident that at first I thought it was a fire siren.

Wirksworth has one of the largest limestone quarries in Europe and the town is stretched across the wounded hill like an antiseptic bandage. Such a grim, workaday place encourages a defiant flippancy that insults its vast history. The location links the Peak District with the pastoral country to the south. Converging roads and the steep market place are reminders that this has been a centre of communications and trade since the Bronze Age. Romans and Anglo-Saxons left their marks on it and sundry other itinerants passed through – less hastily than today's thundering traffic.

The Romans and Saxons exploited the lead mines and Wirksworth became the hub of the industry and the seat of the miners' powerfully independent Barmote or Barmoot Court, which was established in 1288 and was to settle disputes for hundreds of years. The court still meets twice a year, just to honour the tradition. The Moot Hall (not the original) is in a side street behind a side street. You will probably find the place locked, but it contains a brass dish presented to the local miners by Henry VIII in 1513 as a standard measure for lead ore. It also contains a memorial to Elizabeth Evans, a Methodist who preached in the market place, was a familiar figure to the mill-workers at Cromford, or spread the word in local barns or on village greens. She became joint owner of a Wirksworth mill but lost her money. At her own request, no stone marked her grave when she died in 1849.

While pursuing her calling on a prison visit, Mrs Evans heard one of the residents confess to murdering a child. She passed on the story while visiting a niece who lived at Ellastone, south of Ashbourne. Thus was conceived a novel that made Wirksworth as renowned in fiction as it was in fact. The niece was Mary Ann Evans (1819–80), later Mrs Cross, who became even better known under a third name, George Eliot. Like her contemporaries the Brontë sisters, she presumably found it expedient to conceal the fact that she was a woman. Her novel *Adam Bede* (1859) was based on the story her aunt told her. 'Snowfield' has been identified as Wirksworth, 'Oakbourne' as Ashbourne, and 'Hayslope' as Ellastone. Elizabeth Evans was the prototype for Dinah Morris and her husband Samuel the prototype for Seth Bede.

The churchyard graves of Elizabeth and Samuel Evans lie in a peaceful, tucked-away setting that lends itself to fantasy. The churchyard is circular, suggesting prehistoric earthworks, and the site was certainly crossed by at least five ancient tracks – one of them a prehistoric route to Elton, Alport, and Ashford in the Water. The surviving processional ceremony of 'clipping' or 'clypping' the church probably has pagan origins. The church itself, by no means the first on the site, is one of the finest of those mentioned in this book, and is impressive evidence of the prosperous lead-mining era. Its interior walls incorporate fragments of many crude, age-worn carvings, and it is fun trying to sort these out from the rest of the masonry. In the northern wall is a Saxon coffin lid, probably seventh century, with carvings from the life of Christ. The southern wall of the transept has a small sculpture of a twelfth-century lead-miner.

On the Moot Hall are carved panels of the unusual, marble-like stone extracted from Hoptonwood quarries, a mile or so away. Much of the limestone south-west of Middleton is dolomitic, heavily fossilised, and in places decidedly un-British in its climbing challenges. It is also permeated by underground galleries. The Golconda mine (less than half a mile east of Harboro' Rocks), which was worked until 1953, was responsible for about three miles of these galleries. Some large caverns were found in the process. What with the quarries on top and the tunnels below, our ancestors hit this little bit of England with everything they had in the quest for lead and limestone.

In the village of Middleton the mining community of 150 years ago mostly owned their own cottages, had enough pasture for one or two cows, and in bureaucratic records were just as likely to be called 'cowkeepers' as 'miners'. The road from Wirksworth climbs to Middleton and then commands wide views before dropping to the Via Gellia in the Griffe Grange Valley. Below a curve in the road is Mountain Cottage, where D. H. Lawrence lived for a year from 1918 to 1919. The novelist and poet was born and raised at Eastwood, on the A610 between Ambergate and Nottingham.

'Griffe' is an adaptation of a Norse word for a deep and narrow valley. 'Grange' is a familiar reminder of the monastic sheep farms and granaries which were scattered across the land from the twelfth century until the Dissolution in the 1530s. Granges paid their rent in the form of grain. The monks either cleared wasteland or moved in on going concerns, which was less strenuous. Big profits were made by selling the wool to mainland Europe. Griffe Grange, south of the valley, was taken over by the Gell family, who lived at Hopton. The Via Gellia, as you have already guessed, has nothing to do with the Romans. The Gells travelled a lot and had classical tastes. So Philip Gell slapped this incongruous name on a road built around 1800 as a link between Cromford and his lead mines at Carsington. The family's

Two views of Dovedale:
Reynard's Cave (*left*), reached
by a steep ascent from the
river, is a spectacular example
of what can happen when the
roof of a cavern collapses.
The stepping stones (*below*),
at the foot of Thorpe Cloud,
mark the southern extremity
of the gorge

Three Shire Heads, the wild, remote
junction of three counties, was once a
rendezvous and refuge for outlaws and
became equally familiar to prize-fighters

The lonely Jenkin Chapel (St. John's, Saltersford) is unique in its eccentric, farmhouse-style architecture

vanity had an offshoot when a woollen fabric made at a mill in the valley was given the trade name Viyella, a condensed version of Via Gellia.

Like Arkwright at Cromford, the Gells planted trees down the winding gorge in an attempt to restore the natural beauty that had been scarred by industry. On a steep hillside opposite the Pig of Lead Inn – where the Bonsall road joins the Via Gellia – the Ball Eye mine produced ore containing, it was thought, more silver than any other lead in Derbyshire. A skull discovered up there, in the entrance to a cave, is believed to have been that of a mammoth. Early in the nineteenth century there were seven mills stepped up a two-mile stretch of the Via Gellia above Cromford. They took it in turns to use the same stream (reinforced by soughs on its way to the Derwent), which was a crafty and concentrated development of water power. Tufa Cottage is an unusual example of the structural possibilities of this cellular rock. Often formed on moss that gets coated with lime it cannot absorb, tufa has been domesticated as a rockery stone.

At the top end of the Griffe Grange Valley, near Grangemill on the edge of the national park, there is evidence of two vents of a volcano which, millions of years ago, must have drastically rearranged the local geography. To the south and west of Grangemill is a wide area familiar to our nomadic ancestors. Various bumps and wrinkles across the landscape have been found to contain evidence of primitive men, the tools they used, and the animals that roamed around them. Imagine how tough it must have been, scraping a living out of a land like this. The wandering tribes were just getting the hang of farming: 2,000 years or so before anyone attached importance to the use of Bethlehem stables as maternity wards.

The Black Rocks should not be confused with those south of Cromford. To the east, near the site of Griffe Grange, the limestone strata have been heaved, bent, cracked, hacked about, and generally devastated by nature and man in turn. The bizarre convolutions of Harboro' Rocks contain a small cave of slightly overwhelming antiquity (it is more than 1,000ft up, and the water level must once have been higher). Bones have told us that this cave was used by a hyena and a sabre-toothed tiger, and a variety of relics have indicated that man took over the tenancy two or three thousand years BC and stayed on until Roman times, possibly much later. Think about that – and while you are about it, enjoy the view.

To the east, near a minor crossroads, the High Peak trail has two interesting features. One is the Hopton Incline, much of it 1 in 14, which in 1937 was the scene of a fatal derailment. The other is the 113-yard Hopton Tunnel, an unusual feature on this line. To the south is the Bronze Age tumulus of Ivet Low.

The King's Chair, just outside Carsington, is a dolomitic limestone crag topped by a man-made hollow shaped like a throne. It leads us towards Carsington Pasture, where a little cave is hidden away in a depression. It was either here, or in the better-known cave at Harboro' Rocks, that one of England's most famous authors made a startling discovery while touring with friends shortly before his death in 1731. The author was that remarkable non-conformist Daniel Defoe (a surname he adopted in his forties), the son of a London butcher. This one-time hosiery merchant, soldier, convict, and secret agent was a versatile and prolific writer whose works included *Robinson Crusoe*, *Moll Flanders*, and the currently more apposite *Tour Through The Whole Island of Great Britain*. Defoe and his friends found the cave occupied by a miner's wife and five children. Her husband, she said, had been born there. The cave was shelved and equipped with homely things. A hole in the roof (still smoke-stained) served as a chimney. Outside were a few pigs and a cow. While they chatted, Defoe doubtless kept a straight face and nodded in an understanding way. He had travelled widely. *Robinson Crusoe* had been on sale for twelve years. Now its author, at the end of his life, had suddenly been confronted by a situation with many parallels.

If you allow your imagination to wander, do so with your eyes open. Carsington Pasture is riddled with old lead workings and can be hazardous for absent-minded itinerants. Not all the shafts are marked by the cautionary stone 'beehives'.

On its western flank is Brassington ('Branzincton' in the Domesday Book), which was peopled in prehistoric times, stood on a Roman road, and at one time was probably a Scandinavian settlement. Much of the church is twelfth century. The environment of this large, rambling, rather engaging village has been wounded by lead mining and quarrying but has a good deal to offer the historian, the geologist, the botanist, and the climber (there are dolomitic faces at both Brassington and Harboro').

Aldwark, on the other side of the Grangemill–Ashbourne road, was the base for monastic sheep farming at the head of the Griffe Grange Valley. A chambered tomb on Green Low, north of Aldwark, contained pottery, flints, and animal bones dating from about 2000 BC. Its structure must have had much in common with that of the better-known tomb on Minning Low, little more than a mile to the south-west. Sandwiched between the High Peak trail and the softened, intermittent outlines of the same Roman road that went through Brassington, Minning Low was the best neolithic discovery of its kind in the Peak District. A mound obscured by scraggy, wind-worn trees was found to enclose two megalithic tombs. The site also provides impressive if bare views. Unfortunately there is no public access.

An unconventional method of disinterring the past – ploughing – exposed mesolithic tools on a farm near Parwich. This large village straggling round a green was a community long before the Anglo-Saxons turned up. Like Brassington it is sheltered among hills. But Parwich lies on lower ground: so snugly tucked in that, if the mind's eye can conjure up a bay, the place can be pictured as a seaside village of the dim past. Parwich has a wakes week. A wake used to be an all-night vigil in church before certain holy days but the word is now applied to secular festivities.

By contrast with Brassington and Parwich, the communities of Ballidon and Bradbourne are shrunken, ghostly vestiges. The caves on Hipley Hill are like timeless eyes that watched Ballidon grow and wither and die. The village was emptied by monastic landlords in the Middle Ages. There is not much left – a few farms and cottages, a lonely Norman chapel in a field, and a sad assembly of ridges and furrows where houses and streets used to be. At Bradbourne, too, the people were moved out and the sheep were moved in. Bradbourne Hall is supposed to be on the site of a pagan altar and for centuries the place has had the reputation of being haunted. There is some Saxon work in the north wall of the church and in the churchyard is the battered remnant of a Saxon cross dating from AD 800 (give or take fifty years). These 'preaching' crosses, which preceded churches, began to turn up in the Peak District towards the end of the seventh century but were mostly erected in the tenth. The church has a memorial to one of the soldiers who pursued Bonnie Prince Charlie from Ashbourne back to Scotland – Thomas Buckston, who fought at Culloden Moor and lived to be 87.

South of Bradbourne, amid winding lanes and rolling greensward, is the Saxon settlement of Kniveton. What stopped me there was the charming little church. There is a huge sycamore by the gate and an ancient yew outside the crude doorway – its stonework flawed because it was useful for sharpening arrows. The church is basically eleventh or twelfth century. The gallery used to have separate access, up a flight of exterior steps. But about seventy years ago the steps were removed and the doorway sealed. The oaken altar table was formerly in domestic use, probably as a dining table (restless feet have worn grooves in the long rail). The stoup was rescued from the grassy obscurity of the churchyard. Though not unique, the church is a good example of its period – as is Kniveton's little 1832 chapel.

Much of the road from Wirksworth to Carsington, Kniveton and Ashbourne follows the course of the Romans' Hereward Street. It would be a pity to regard Ashbourne as no more than the southern entrance to the Peak District in general and Dovedale in particular. 'Essenburne' in the Domesday Book, Ashbourne was destroyed by fire in 1252 and has had a thoroughly eventful history. In a period of less than 200 years, for example, it was directly associated with the Civil War, Bonnie Prince Charlie, Dr Samuel Johnson, the Napoleonic Wars, and the origins of the Salvation Army. Not bad for starters.

During the Civil War, Parliamentary troops were bombarding the church with cannon-balls (the dents are still there) when a deputation of townsfolk turned up and asked them to stop it – which they did, doubtless because they were somewhat dumbfounded to be asked so nicely. A hundred years later who should turn up but Bonnie Prince Charlie and his Highlanders, like a vanguard for today's army of tourists.

Charles Edward Stuart (1720–88) began and ended his life in Rome. In 1745 he quietly made his way to Scotland to lead a conspiracy of the Scots and the French against the English monarchy. His father, the son of James II, had tried the same thing in 1715 but had come unstuck. Bonnie Prince Charlie did better. He was an intelligent, dashing young man of considerable charm, and the clans were duly impressed when they gathered around his royal standard at Glenfinnan, on the shore of Loch Shiel. That was in August. By December they were in Ashbourne, having diverted the attention of the English troops – hurriedly recalled from Flanders – with a fake attack on Congleton. The Highlanders probably chose the western route round the Peak District (via Macclesfield and Leek) because they had nasty memories of the eastern flank: five generations and 200 years earlier the Prince's ancestress, Mary Queen of Scots, had spent a lot of time in detention there.

The Prince stopped in Ashbourne to eat at an inn where a shop now stands, by Compton Bridge. He was soon back. The march to London got no farther than Derby. There our hero was persuaded, after much argument, that he was on a hiding to nothing – that there was an imminent danger of his army becoming a thin slice of Scottish meat in a thick English sandwich. One can sympathise with the man. He had been disappointed in his hopes that the French would also invade England, and that English Jacobites would swarm to his support. He was not to know, as you and I do, that the men of the North of England are not the kind to rush rapturously towards bagpipes and go into battle on behalf of a foreigner wearing a tartan skirt and a feathered bonnet.

Anyway, they retreated. The Prince and his officers spent a night as house guests at Ashbourne Hall (its remnants are now incorporated in a library). Then the Highlanders were pursued to Scotland. Four months later, though weakened by weariness and desertions, they decided to stand their ground on Culloden Moor. But they were outnumbered, outsmarted, and slaughtered. That terrible defeat killed the Jacobite cause – the Jacobites were supporters of the Stuarts, particularly James II and his descendants – and ended the clan system by breaking the hereditary and legal power of the chieftains. It also marked the beginning of the most romantic chapter in the Prince's story: the five months in which he was hunted throughout the Highlands and Hebrides, escaping with the help of a young lady called Flora Macdonald. Whereupon he fled to the European mainland and the consolations of a mistress, a daughter, a wife, and the bottle.

One of Bonnie Prince Charlie's contemporaries, Dr Samuel Johnson, was the literary giant of his day, though his enduring reputation rests chiefly on his dictionary and on the biography written by his young friend James Boswell. Ashbourne saw a lot of these two because Johnson enjoyed the hospitality provided there by a friend from his schooldays,

Dr John Taylor, whose interests included the breeding of cattle and bulldogs for show purposes.

During the Napoleonic Wars, French prisoners were accommodated at Ashbourne, which was regarded as adequately remote. The next event of note, in 1829, was the birth of Catherine Mumford. She followed the example of Elizabeth Evans by becoming a public preacher, which was a bold thing for a woman to do, and helped her husband – William Booth – to found the Salvation Army. A memorial bust to 'The Army Mother' stands in a park near the centre of the town. More prominently eye-catching is the unusual sign outside the Green Man and Black's Head (a conjunction that arose about 1826 when two inns were amalgamated). On a beam that spans the main road is a painting of a man in green on a shooting trip, and above this is a two-faced model of a blackamoor's head. He is grinning cheerfully towards traffic advancing along the one-way street but, conversely, is glumly soulful as the same traffic recedes.

Behind the inn is a car park where the renowned 'football' match is begun by tossing the ball into the crowd. Such contests were widely popular around 1400 but Ashbourne's, played on Shrove Tuesday and Ash Wednesday, is an isolated survival of the tradition. Play continues from two o'clock until a goal is scored or darkness intervenes. The teams are the 'Up'ards', who live north of the Henmore Brook and play upstream, and the 'Down'ards', who live south of it. Goals are scored by banging the ball on Sturston Mill or on a stone marking the site of Clifton Mill, about three miles away. Thousands watch and hundreds take part, often knee deep in the brook. The ball can be thrown, carried, kicked, or whatever. But the match often seems to consist of a prolonged communal hug, and the scope for damage to participants and property is awful – which explains why this heaving roughhouse is no longer started in the market place.

Ashbourne has had a market since 1257. The sloping, cobbled market place has been reduced by building but retains much of the stimulating character it must have had in the days of travelling shows, bull-baiting, cock-fighting, coiners, preachers, stagecoach traffic, off-duty highwaymen and Bonnie Prince Charlie optimistically proclaiming his father king.

Beyond Dig (formerly 'Ditch') Street is the elegant Georgian dignity of Church Street, where Johnson used to stay with his friend in the Mansion opposite Queen Elizabeth's Grammar School. The church lies on low ground and this lessens the impact of the 212ft spire, which also has to compete with the chimney of the Nestlé factory for aerial prominence. St Oswald's is the third church on this site, was dedicated in 1241, and has a double piscina from that period. There are few Peak District churches that can challenge its grandeur; but like so many of these large cruciform structures it has something of the character of an indoor crossroads, the four segments detracting from the unity of the whole. In the northern transept is a huddle of nine effigies, members of the Cokayne and Boothby families who lived in turn at Ashbourne Hall. If you happen to be there alone in failing light, the chapel is like a slightly nerve-chilling ecclesiastical warehouse and can play tricks on the imagination. But these are remarkable tombs. The most engaging effigy, in a sleeping posture, is that of the only child of a broken marriage, Penelope Boothby. She was painted by Sir Joshua Reynolds at the age of three and died in 1791 at the age of five. On the southern side of the nave is a memorial window to the Turnbull sisters. When a lamp exploded in their father's hands they rushed to help him; but their flimsy gowns caught fire and they were burned to death. Note, too, the pulpit, which has inlays of Castleton's famous Blue John stone.

There is much more that could be said about Ashbourne: about its location, linking highland and lowland Britain and the trade between them; about its importance on the old Manchester–London coaching route; about its tradition of breeding shire-horses (the annual show also has a class for the mule, that self-willed offspring of horse and donkey); about its toy museum; and about such products as embroidered lace, knitted stockings, corsets, gingerbread, and bottled mineral water. But we have demonstrated that Ashbourne is much more than a doorway to the Peak District.

Across Hanging Bridge (so called because some of the Scottish rebels were hanged there in 1745) is Mayfield, which was the home of an Irish poet, Thomas Moore (1779–1852), while he was writing the oriental romance *Lalla Rookh*. On opposite banks of the Dove are Mapleton, with its quaint little church, and what is left of the medieval village of Oke-over – evacuated to make way for a deer park. Okeover Hall and the church were plundered by the Jacobites on their way to Ashbourne. Fenny Bentley, on the Buxton road, has a fifteenth-century tower and, in the church across the road, the shrouded effigies of Thomas Beresford, his wife, and their twenty-one children. This prolific family, plus retainers, provided Henry V with a complete troop of horsemen who fought at Agincourt in 1415.

Fenny Bentley has some attractive cottages and prepares us, mentally, for the mellow neatness of Tissington, an attractive example of the many estate villages built for the work-force necessary to maintain the properties of wealthy landowners. Places like Tissington and its industrial counter-part at Cromford, eight miles away, do not justify the social conditions that created them. But their inhabitants benefited – and so did posterity.

Approached via a gate and an avenue of limes, Tissington is like a model carefully planned to look haphazard. Except for the fact that the nearest pub is on the A515, half a mile away, it has all the expected features: a green, a pond, a church, roadside lawns, a tea room (in the old school), and the Hall where the gentry live. Yet it is so litterlessly tidy in its attractive propriety, so subdued in its serenity, that the lack of vitality induces a tendency to talk in muted tones as if in some kind of museum. I was delighted to apply my brakes in the interests of a boy who, satisfying some inner compulsion, was running backwards up a lane before opening a gate for a rosy-cheeked girl shepherding sheep and chubby, black-faced lambs. In its context his exuberance was as refreshing as a sudden breeze on a day heavy with heat.

Tissington has five wells and in a festival beginning on Ascension Day these are dressed in floral and botanical bounty. Tissington's was the prototype for all well dressings and is still the most renowned. It may have had pagan origins. It may have been born when the village was spared during the Black Death. It may commemorate the fact that the wells never failed during the drought of 1615, when there were only three showers in nineteen weeks and sheep and cattle starved to death because the grass withered. But the first festival actually recorded was in 1758.

Like that at Kniveton, the doorway of the twelfth-century church still bears the grooves worn when archers were sharpening their arrows. The pulpit is a canopied 'double-decker' and the font has unusual human and animal carvings. Tissington Hall – adorned with battlements, parapets, chimneys like turrets, and a clock that rings a bell – is very much the ancestral home. Built in 1609 and later extended, it has always been occupied by the Fitzherberts, lords of the manor since the fifteenth century.

The conversation round the family dinner table must have been particularly interesting in the 1780s, because Alleyne Fitzherbert, a diplomat, was touring the Crimea with Catherine the Great while Maria Anne, widow of Thomas Fitzherbert, was settling down to a form of marriage with the artistic but dissolute Prince of Wales, later George IV. Mrs Fitzherbert, née Smythe, was a famous beauty and had a long life (1756–1837) but made a frustrating choice of husbands. By the age of 25 she had twice been widowed, and her marriage to the Prince in 1785 was invalid. He was under 25 at the time and, legally, needed his father's consent. This was refused (by marrying Mrs Fitzherbert, a Roman

Catholic, the Prince would have forfeited his right to the crown). The Prince was haplessly married to a German princess, Caroline of Brunswick. Mrs Fitzherbert remained his only serious attachment and continued to enjoy a respected if ambiguous status. The liaison lasted until 1803.

Between Tissington and Bradbourne, several footpaths converge on Lea Hall without apparent cause. They do so because this was the site of a hamlet that was deserted in the sixteenth century when the land was converted from arable farming to a pasture for sheep. To the north-west Alsop en le Dale is the sort of place you could drive through without noticing it was there. But Alsop is a pleasing example of the quiet, grey, durable upland settlements scattered over the Peak District. Snugly ensconced within the unusually thick walls of the Norman church are sixteen small pews which could accommodate about sixty people.

But on leaving Ashbourne most newcomers will make for Dovedale: initially for Thorpe, a name that suggests Danish origins. The village sprawls across a hillside east of the confluence of Dove and Manifold, and has a little church built in the twelfth century. Thorpe Cloud (in old English 'clud' meant 'a rock or hill') is a conical, gracefully striking specimen of the fossilised coral reefs formed on the bed of an ancient sea. The Dove is flanked by several such hills, particularly between Crowdecote and Hollinsclough, and in shape if not in size they satisfy the modern connotations of the word 'peak'. Thorpe Cloud is a 942ft bulwark over the southern entrance to Dovedale, and is worth climbing because of its superb view of Dovedale's geological and botanical wonderland and the landscape in which this is set. There are indications that the Dove once flowed at a higher level down a broad valley until the river gradually eroded the existing gorge.

Dovedale, little more than three miles long, lies between Milldale in the north and the spot where the Dove is reinforced by the Manifold. The famous bit, less than two miles of it, is the wooded ravine between the stepping stones at the foot of Thorpe Cloud and the cave-like Dove Holes. You will have to get it out of your system sooner or later. So do the job thoroughly: park at the southern end, walk Dovedale both ways in order to savour the views from each direction, and climb Thorpe Cloud so that the picture can be put in its frame. Look out for the flowers, the plants, the ash woods, and the birds (you may even see a kingfisher). Listen to the water music at the artificial weirs that form pools where the trout and grayling gather. In short, keep your eyes, your ears, and your heart open.

Upstream from the stepping stones, the height on the left known as Dovedale Castle is succeeded by the outcrops of the Twelve Apostles. These are backed by the rare sight of ash woods that regenerate naturally – best viewed from the grassy spur called Lover's Leap, which is worth the additional scramble because of its wide prospect of Dovedale's astonishing limestone jungle. Back in the gorge, the walker passes the upraised fingers of Tissington Spires and is then confronted by the geological oddity of Reynard's Cave high on the eastern bank. It is amazing what water and weather and a few million years can do. The massive, detached arch of rock was the mouth of a cavern until the roof fell in. A vestigial cave remains, farther back, plus a few fissures and tunnels. The views across to Jacob's Ladder are spectacular. But the exploration of Reynard's Cave, like the ascent to it, can be hazardous. There is a cautionary tale of an Irish dean who tried to go up there on horseback, with a young lady riding pillion. The horse slipped, all three tumbled down the slope, and the dean died from his injuries and was buried at Ashbourne. So make sure that young children, dogs, and those afflicted by infirmity or vertigo are safely tethered and left to graze by the river before you go gadding up the hill.

Dovedale then becomes a defile that would be claustrophobic if its walls were higher. The path ducks under Lion's

Head Rock – which takes its name from its profile – by means of a raised wooden sidewalk that ends where a stream tumbles out of a little cave. A rocky path below crumbled piles of limestone detritus leads to Ilam Rock, which rises sheer from the water's edge like a slice of the world's crust that was left over when everyone had been served. The southern face is so smoothly perpendicular that it might have been severed from the mother rock by a giant cleaver. Pickering Tor, on the right, is like a natural fortress. Across the river is Hurt's Wood (a family name), another example of an ancient type of woodland. The gorge terminates where the river swings east between the crag called Raven's Tor and the Dove Holes, two arched recesses that were hollowed out when the water level was higher.

And that, essentially, is the tourist trap that served as a model for George Eliot's 'Eagledale'. There is not much of it, and other dales may surpass it in particular features. The unique quality of Dovedale is its compact diversity. There is something different and interesting to be seen at every twist in the river and at every season of the year. It is as if the Almighty had searched His stockroom for beautiful and bizarre bits and pieces and then arranged them – in one small area – with an artistic genius that gave the dramatic contrasts a breathtaking harmony. The topography of Dovedale is a mess touched by magic.

The trouble with Dovedale is that too many people go there expecting too much – and cannot avoid one another because the place is so cramped. Imagine the human contents of Terminal 3 at Heathrow transferred into a lovely natural environment and you will appreciate that going to Dovedale cannot be construed as getting away from it all. But some people enjoy crowds. The rest of us can tramp through Dovedale at dawn or dusk or outside the holiday season and be grateful for what we receive in the way of birdsong and buttercups.

My most recent visits were on two grey March days

after a long, harsh winter. Retained water was still spilling across a battered landscape stained by dirty patches of snow – sadly marooned rags from the lovely white mantle that had given us months of Christmas-card views. My wife and I were 'underwhelmed' by the introduction: Lin Dale was not wearing its yellow summer dress; red signs strewn across the hillside indicated that when flags were flying, the imprudent might be shot; and there was no escape from the squelching mud and wide-streaming water. There were no sheep about, so we freed the dogs and let them take a bath on the run. Down in Dovedale, the stepping stones were submerged. A disillusioned, retreating walker paused in the morass and muttered cynically:

'It's rather like Lathkill Dale. When you've seen one, you've seen them all . . .'

A fortnight later I returned alone, parked at Milldale (where the facilities for doing so are limited), and walked Dovedale both ways. It was less animated this time, but still mucky. An Old English Sheepdog, legs brown with filth, emerged from the trees and tried to shake off the clinging wetness. It was as if a gust of wind had hit a waterfall. I passed the time of day with a grim-faced rambler whose trousers looked like the undersides of two mudguards.

'There's muck and watter everywheer tha goes,' he observed mournfully. 'Can't mek out which is t' path and which is t' bloody river.'

The round trip completed, I returned to the suddenly widening valley at Dove Holes, turned uphill beside the rugged outline of The Nabs, and skirted Hanson Grange. This was one of several monastic sheep farms in the area. Newton Grange was the hub of a much earlier settlement, going back at least as far as the Saxons but long since reduced to little more than a few farms. There are a few ancient burial mounds about, too. While ruminating on all this and plodding past Hanson Grange, I was brought sharply up to date when a chestnut pony, looking for a playmate, came racing across the field at an alarming velocity. He pranced around and kept nudging me in the back in that potentially flattening way ponies have. There were lambs in the next field. So recently cosy in the womb, they were now sniffing the bitter wind, looking at the rain and the banked snow, and wondering what the hell had gone wrong.

Boots swished through wet grass as I went steeply downhill to rejoin the gurgling, chuckling Dove. When approached from the hills – and the options are restricted – the secluded hamlet of Milldale is like a film set or a jumbled assembly of doll's houses. The Methodist chapel is, in fact, no larger than a modest living room. The link with Dovedale is Viator's Bridge, a quaint little structure on which packhorses trod a straight and narrow path in the seventeenth century. It was from this bridge, while walking to Beresford Hall with Charles Cotton, that Izaak Walton saw the Dove for the first time. These two men, especially Cotton, were responsible for the initial burst of lyrical publicity that gave Dovedale its exaggerated reputation – and, perversely, encouraged genera-tions of tourists to erode the idyllic enchantment that so moved the original publicists.

Walton (1593–1683) was a Stafford man and Cotton (1630–87) was born by the Dove, at Beresford Hall, and spent most of his life there. They were an oddly assorted couple bound in firm friendship by common enthusiasms for angling and literature. Walton, almost thirty-seven years the elder, had been an ironmonger. A gentle man and a devout Chris-tian, he became a charming writer and produced five bio-graphies, but is best known for his pleasantly instructive book *The Compleat Angler, or The Contemplative Man's Recreation.* Cotton, a fast-living squire, gambled away his own money and that of two wives. He was always in debt but was so spirited, so affably personable, that even his creditors could not help liking him – though by 1681 the situation had be-come so tricky that he had to sell Beresford Hall. Cotton wrote verses and parodies and translated Montaigne's essays. But his literary stature rests chiefly on the dialogue between Piscator (the angler) and Viator (the traveller) that forms the second part of *The Compleat Angler*. Cotton's contribution, incorporated in the fifth edition in 1676, was written in ten days at the request of Walton, who was then 83. It remains the authoritative work on fly-fishing in the upper reaches of the Dove. Cotton was also a self-appointed advertising agent for his own corner of England. In 1681 he produced a laudatory if commonplace poem entitled 'The Wonders of the Peak'.

A mile from Milldale, in the church at Alstonefield (Aelfstan's Feld), is the ugly olive-grey family pew built for Cotton's father. St Peter's contains such a variety of pews and benches that it is like a furniture showroom. It is an odd place altogether. The nave and chancel are not in line. The pillars on either side of the nave differ in style and their bases are hidden – indicating, like the low position of the double piscina in the chancel, that the floor is higher than it used to be. The imposing 'two-decker' pulpit was originally a 'three-decker'. Near the door is an old chest that once accommodated valuables. It had three locks and the vicar and the church-wardens had one key each, which meant that the chest could only be opened in the presence of all three. Behind the font is the bowl of a Saxon font (dug up in the churchyard) and fragments of Anglo-Saxon or Viking crosses are built into the walls in the area of the porch. There are more of these in the south porch, which has an unusual stone roof. St Peter's is probably the third church built on this site and its crosses are as eclectic as its pews. But from the churchyard gate the most obviously unusual feature is the chequered pattern of sandstone and local limestone. Alongside, the 1587 manor house is now a farm.

An engaging upland village, Alstonefield lies on the junction of what are now minor roads. It used to have a market and was the centre of a large parish, but its stature diminished as that of Ashbourne and Hartington grew. The George, which has a craft centre, was a sixteenth-century coaching inn. I popped in to acquire internal and external warmth. The latter hope was to some extent thwarted by a rotund old retriever who looked as if it (sex uninvestigated) had been lying in front of the fireplace for centuries. Perhaps they built the inn round it.

East of Alstonefield the Dove flows through a deep and often bare ravine towards Coldeaton, a settlement that died in the Middle Ages. A much earlier death – a pagan cremation – was exposed by the excavation of human remains, fragments of bone combs, and twenty-eight bone counters for playing some kind of game. To the north-east, the Tissington Trail passes through the Coldeaton Cutting, which was a major engineering feat in its time. South and north of Coldeaton you may find herb robert embellishing the screes – or 'slitherbanks' – of Iron Tors and the dry gorge of Biggin Dale. Meadow sweet, meadow cranesbill, and celandine adorn the meadows by the Dove as it wanders round the reef formation of Gratton Hill into Wolfscote Dale, itself a striking example of the contorting effect of upheavals in the bed of that ancient sea. Wolves used to roam through this narrow, steep-walled cleft between Gratton Hill and Wolfscote Hill.

A packhorse bridge separates Wolfscote Dale from the delightfully wooded and flowery Beresford Dale, a minigorge with weirs, pools, and strangely shaped rocks. Some like it even better than Dovedale. Much of the woodland was originally planted on Cotton's initiative. He is said to have evaded his creditors by hiding in a cave at the southern end of the dale, or in other riverside nooks and crannies. Beresford Hall was reduced to ruins in 1856 and there is little left of it now. But at the northern end of the woods, in a lovely spot on private ground, the 'fishing house' built by Cotton in 1674 – with the initials IWCC over the doorway – was restored in the nineteenth century. Nearby is Pike Pool, where a slim, spire-like rock soars from the water like a sculptor's impression of a gigantic fish rising to the bait.

At this northern extremity of the Dove's prettiest and most

diverse reaches is Hartington, well known to tourists in general and anglers in particular. Granted a market charter in 1203, the oldest on record in the Peak District, it no longer has a market but retains the large open area – complete with pond – where it was held. Hartington used to be the hub of a thriving agricultural area and a parish divided into 'quarters' that stretched sixteen miles from Alsop en le Dale to Buxton. It had links with lead and copper mines and was sandwiched between two stations three miles apart, at Hulme End and 'Hartington'. The latter station was in fact at the top of Hand Dale. Workers preparing the foundations for a viaduct broke through into an old mine and found skeletons, presumably those of trapped miners. The 'Hartington' signal box has been retained as an information point on the Tissington Trail. One wintry morning I met two ladies who were labouring up the steep steps with crates of hand-outs in readiness for the holiday season.

Hartington Hall, rebuilt in 1611 and restored in 1862, is now a youth hostel. The church has some interesting gargoyles. And Hartington produces Britain's finest cheese . . .

The strange thing about Stilton is that although it was named after a Huntingdonshire village (where it was served at a local inn and gained a reputation among travellers), it was never made there. That distinction belongs to Leicestershire, Derbyshire, and Nottinghamshire. The Hartington factory was set up by a Leicestershire family, the Nuttalls, and now makes 1,600 tons of cheese a year: roughly 88 per cent Blue Stilton, 10 per cent Stilton, and a little Blue Wensleydale. More than a gallon of pasteurised milk (the process took its name from Louis Pasteur, the French chemist) is needed to make a pound of cheese. The blue veins are caused by air penetrating the cheese – through holes made by stainless steel needles – in the regulated temperature and humidity of the store where the cheese matures.

For three nights I stayed at the Charles Cotton Hotel. This experience was enlivened by candlelit drinking during an electricity failure; a snowstorm (on 28th March, if you please); news of drifts and blocked roads; and relevant conversational asides from my hosts to the effect that one 'overnight' guest had recently been stuck there for three, that no post had arrived for four days, and that a local invalid had died before an ambulance could get through to him.

They fed me well, though. I never felt any need for lunch, other than the kind of cold drink that makes a man feel warm; because breakfasts and dinners at the Charles Cotton were of a size that did not permit intervening consumption. One grilled breakfast included an unusual component – a segment of oatcake. I was interested in what it had to say to me, but was not converted.

In the bar was a man from Halifax who said he drove to Hartington and back three times a week and had been making the trip for eighteen years. He did not mind the drive, he said, as long as he got back to Halifax. It was 'a grand run – all of it'. No, he could not recommend any inns farther north in the Peak District. 'If I'm within an hour and a half's drive, I'll stay here. This is the place – here' (emphasising his point by stabbing a finger towards the floor). But the best moment at the Charles Cotton occurred when a local lad ordered his beer, examined it with anticipatory rapture, and observed: 'I like to see a head on me beer. You can tell it's right way up if it's got a head on it.'

Hartington was built from a mixture of limestone and gritstone (easier to work). A more obvious hint that the landscape is approaching a change of character is provided in the Dove valley, which expands as if coming up for air. The ridge separating the Dove from the Manifold rises to 1,247ft on Sheen Hill. The village of Sheen is renowned for its tug of war expertise and a medieval burial ground. To the north-east, by the A515, the beautifully named hamlet of Parsley Hay was a child of the CHPR era (at 1,150ft its station was among the highest in England) and now marks the junction of the High Peak and Tissington Trails. Between

Sheen and Parsley Hay, on meadows alongside the Dove, are the grassy banks and mounds known as Pilsbury Castle. Its history is mysterious because of the dearth of evidence, but speculation suggests that a wooden Norman castle may have been built here on the site of an earthwork from Saxon or even Iron Age times. Anyway, it is a remote and charming spot – and somewhat haunting if your imagination happens to be on that wavelength.

One wintry morning I drove from Hartington up Long Dale and then north-west along slushy minor roads leading nowhere in particular. The roads were just tracks between intrusive banks of snow. The fields were dressed in white. The drive was slightly hazardous, but desolately impressive. Suddenly, as the highway swung right and dipped towards Crowdecote, there sprang into view one of the most dramatic sights I have come across in the Peak District. Lumped massively along the north-eastern flank of the Dove was a range of reef hills that – making due allowance for the flattering distortion of scale, a trick played by the snow on the tops – was like something straight out of the Alps. Such scenes are etched for ever on the minds of those with an affinity for high, lonely places.

The heights are High Wheeldon, Aldery Cliff, Hitter Hill, Parkhouse Hill, Chrome Hill, and Hollins Hill, with High Edge and Upper Edge looming beyond. Imagine that lot at the bottom of the sea, as they once were, assembling layers of fossils and proudly pushing up peaks for our future delectation. There is some gritstone about, too, reminding us that we are close to another kind of Peak District.

Pottery dating from more than 1,000 years BC was found in a cave on High Wheeldon. But in a prehistoric sense the star of the show is a narrow, steep cave in Dowel Dale, between Parkhouse Hill and Chrome Hill. This turned out to be a compendium of archaeological goodies from the palaeolithic, mesolithic, and neolithic periods – that is, from the nomadic hunters of more than a million years ago to the relatively settled communities of two or three thousand years BC. The finds included flint blades, bits of charcoal and pottery, remnants of possibly ten human burials, and bones of fish, water birds, early animals, and more familiar creatures such as the red deer, sheep, goat, pig, and dog. The prolonged popularity of this cave, plus the nature of some of its contents, suggests that the basin between Parkhouse Hill and Chrome Hill was an unusually inviting site and probably contained a lake or at least a large pond. Nowadays the upper part of Dowel Dale is dry. But near Greensides Farm are several swallow holes (or 'swallets') which enable water flowing down from the hills to dive underground. It reappears as a spring near Dowel Farm and then runs half a mile into the Dove.

Crowdecote is a corruption of 'Cruda's Cot' (Cruda was a Saxon landowner and a cot is a modest cottage or shelter). The Pack Horse Inn, a charming little place, is adorned by an old pack saddle – with a row of tiny brass bells that presumably served as the equivalent of a car horn or the chimes of an ice-cream van. Less than two miles away, at Earl Sterndale, is a pub called The Quiet Woman. The sign is a headless lady in a green gown who supposedly represents a nagging wife known as 'Chattering Charteris'. The story goes that her henpecked husband eventually decapitated her, whereupon the approving villagers had a whip round to buy a headstone and gave him the balance.

I had to step over a stout old collie, lying in the porch and gazing unblinkingly at the wind and the rain and the backcloth of snow.

'Not in t' way, is he?' called a voice from inside.

'No. But he must be daft or dead to stay out there in this weather.'

Earl Sterndale is a quarrying village. During the Second World War its church was burnt down, except for the stonework, when hit by an incendiary bomb. The Germans were aiming for a massive explosives dump in a disused quarry near the Buxton road, and a premature bomb fell on the church. Between Earl Sterndale and the A515 is Dow Low, disfigured by huge quarries and a dusty grey 'village' of works buildings. This industrial mess is so grotesque, so much at odds with its environment, that it looks like something out of science fiction.

West of Earl Sterndale, at the foot of a rocky little dale, is Glutton, which may have been a settlement on a bay in the days when the water level was much higher. The name came not from any notorious gourmand but from the biggest of the weasel family, the wolverine or glutton, a voracious predator found in Arctic or sub-Arctic regions. Farther up the Dove is Hollinsclough, which is built on gritstone among a striking array of limestone hills that give it the character of a remote mountain hamlet. The interior of the small bethel has cliff-like patterns reflecting the same image.

The sources of the Dove and Manifold are only half a mile apart, just east of the A53 Buxton–Leek road. The Dove rises from a spring near Dove Head, the Manifold from a swamp near one of England's highest inns, the Traveller's Rest. The distance between the two rivers is never much more than three miles – usually half that – and they finally unite between Ilam and Thorpe. Neither is easily approached by road. These are rivers for the walker and the angler. The Manifold is the less accessible and is also less spectacular in terms of rock and woodland scenery. But seclusion is part of its charm and in many ways the scenery in its larger, more open valley matches that of the Dove in quality if not in kind.

Between Hollinsclough and Longnor is Moss Carr, a marshy hollow that drains into the Manifold and has some interesting flora that includes the bogbean, cranberry, marsh cinquefoil, and even a branch of the adaptable orchid family.

Longnor is a plain, compact, yet higgledy-piggledy place with dark old gritstone houses and a significant location. It stands on the east–west boundary between the bright greenery of the limestone country and the sombre browns and greys of the gritstone landscape; on a ridge between the Dove and the Manifold where they are only three-quarters of a mile apart; and on a busy junction of minor roads that wander into verdant emptiness. To some extent it remains an oasis in an upland desert, a role forced upon it by an expanding farming community towards the end of the eighteenth century, when new farms were taming the open moorland. Longnor is no longer a market town. But high on the market hall, overlooking the square, is a notice concerning the tolls salesmen had to pay at markets and fairs in 1903. And there is still a wakes festival.

A decade or so ago Longnor attracted international attention with a no-smoking campaign that inspired much devious deceit. A more enduring source of renown lies in the churchyard. I refer not to the building, which looks like a converted warehouse; nor to a yew that seems once to have been disembowelled but is nevertheless flourishing; but to a memorial stone that stands among other upright slabs down a dip to the right from the path between gate and church. This stone concerns William Billinge, who spent 112 years travelling 150 yards by a circuitous and adventurous route.

He was born in 1679 in a cornfield at Fawfieldhead (moorland country to the south-west) and died 150 yards away in January 1791, having lived through seven reigns. A soldier for most of his active life, Billinge took part in the capture of Gibraltar in 1704, was wounded by a musket shot in the thigh when serving under the Duke of Marlborough at the Battle of Ramillies in Belgium in 1706, and helped to suppress the Jacobite rebellions of 1715 and 1745. At least, that is what we are told. But to do a few sums is to colour awe with scepticism. Because it seems that Billinge was born in a field in January, at an altitude around 1,000ft, and was still soldiering on sixty-six years later. Possible, but unlikely. To give birth to a baby in a cornfield (as distinct from conceiving one there) must have been eccentric even in those days. The idea of a heavily pregnant woman wandering about a field in January, at such a height and in such a climate, hardly bears thinking about. And are we expected to believe in a 66-year-old fighting soldier?

But wait. The British calendar was revised in 1752, which throws a little confusion on the already vague date of birth. And my bedside reading during this sceptical period revealed a second example of a soldier on active service at the age of 66. This was the Governor of Kentucky, who retained 'the vigour and zeal of youth' when commanding an important position during Britain's defeat at the Battle of the Thames (the one in Ontario) in 1813.

So let us give William Billinge the benefit of the doubt. He was a fine advertisement for a military career based on a cornfield.

In the last few decades many visitors were attracted to Longnor by the reputation of an eccentric versifier who was familiar to the regulars at four conveniently bunched inns. Two ladies in the Cheshire Cheese told me about him.

'If he met you and you came back next week, he'd have written a poem about you. "Wicked Will", they called him. Just died: seventy-five, he was.'

'That winter finished him. And the life he led. Often he wouldn't go out till ten. Then he'd go the rounds. He raked out, as they say.'

'They found him on his doorstep. Must have been there since midnight. Had the key in his hand.'

South of Longnor, at a T-junction along the fork to Reaps Moor, is an isolated building with a rare design. The northern end is a dwelling house. The ground floor of the southern end was formerly a schoolroom, now in general use for parish functions, and the first floor is a chapel that still has a monthly service. To the south-east is Hulme End, originally a Scandinavian settlement, later the terminus of the Leek and Manifold Light Railway (note the Light Railway Hotel), and now just a farming hamlet. 'Hulm' is a Danish word, indicating an island or waterside meadow. In this case the water is the

Manifold's. If you are well shod and feeling strong, Hulme End can be the start and finish of a long but consistently delightful walk – down the Manifold to Ilam and then up the Dove to the top of Beresford Dale. Such a ramble would be too much for children. But much of it can be enjoyed piecemeal with the help of a car.

Tucked into the valley south-west of Hulme End is the hamlet of Ecton, which used to bob along the rural mainstream – it was well known for copper and lead mining, a dairy, a button factory, and a railway station – but has long since been tossed aside like a forlorn piece of jetsam drained of commercial value. The copper mines on the 1,212ft Ecton Hill were concentrated on its northern projection near Apes Tor, where the limestone had already been folded and twisted by prehistoric earth movements. One shaft, descending about 1,400ft, was among the deepest in Europe. These mines were worked from the seventeenth century until the 1880s, when the falling price of copper made production unprofitable. In 1786 the yield was about 4,000 tons. In those days the mines employed 300 people, give or take a few. The men worked night and day in six-hour shifts underground. Too often, mangled dead were brought up – killed by falls or blasting (these were the first English mines to use gunpowder). Women broke up the ore, and children did lighter work, preparing the precious stuff for its rough journey along hilly tracks. The profits from all this enabled the Dukes of Devonshire to improve Chatsworth and build The Crescent at Buxton. The industry made a mess of a lovely stretch of the Manifold. But the valley works have gone and little remains of the miners' settlement except for some cottages up the hill near a folly: a 'castle' built in the 1930s with a copper spire to remind us of Ecton's industrial past.

The Manifold is flanked by mostly bare countryside rising beyond 1,000ft. This gives the scattered villages a ruggedly distinctive character. The churches of Warslow and Upper Elkstone are galleried and Upper Elkstone's two-decker pulpit has a canopy, which could be construed as a vote of no confidence in the rainproof qualities of the roof. Another isolated, charming old village is Butterton ('ton' or 'tun' is a common Anglo-Saxon suffix indicating an enclosure, farm, or hamlet), which straggles over a hillside and, at its southern extremity, has a narrow ford over Hoo Brook, a tributary of the Manifold.

The octagonal spire of Grindon church, farther south, is a landmark for miles. Just inside the church door is a vividly simple little tapestry hinting at a moorland crucifixion. This is a memorial to eight RAF men who were killed when their aircraft crashed on Grindon Moor while bringing emergency supplies to upland communities isolated by deep snow during the 1947 blizzard. Grindon is one of those high places that, as if heaving towards it, seem to have more than their share of sky. But the oddest thing about it, at least in my experience, is the seventeenth-century Cavalier Inn. I called one day at noon but was told: 'Sorry. We don't open till Easter.'

The flow of traffic and water in this area is interesting. If you use the same kind of map as I do you will notice that the roads are all minor (dictionary: 'comparatively unimportant') and tend to be emblazoned with black chevrons identifying steep gradients. A drive from Grindon to Weag's Bridge and Wetton will suffice as an example of what the cartographers are trying to tell us. The Manifold suddenly begins to behave in an odd way and, superficially, becomes no more than an occasional river. Unless the weather has been exceptionally wet, the Manifold drains out of sight as if through a sunken limestone colander. Just below Wettonmill it is little more than a trickle. Then the river vanishes and, except for a few pools, runs underground through four or five miles of attractively wooded scenery. It gradually reappears between Rushley Bridge and the grounds of Ilam Hall and, as if nothing had happened, reassumes the fluvial conventions until it joins the Dove.

The eccentric beauty of the Manifold and Dove valleys

hereabouts should not blind us to the intervening charms of the landscape, from Wetton and Alstonefield in the north to Ilam in the south. Wetton – huddled round an inn and a church that has an exterior staircase to the belfry – combines an exhilarating environment with historic rarities. The village has Anglian origins but on its edge, at Borough Fields, excavations exposed an older settlement, probably Roman. Burial mounds on Wetton Low contained thirteen human skeletons and the bones of animals, including oxen and deer. All that dates from about 1600BC. But we have to go back to neanderthal man, roughly 50,000 years earlier, in order to envisage the inhabitants of the small, high caves near Wettonmill.

The best-known prehistoric landmark is Thor's Cave, a spectacular, gaping hole in a huge crag over the Manifold. In addition to an assortment of animal bones and evidence of cooking, this cave contained flint arrowheads, iron adzes, bronze bracelets and brooches, and ancient pottery and coins. Its history is comparable with that of the cave in Dowel Dale, spanning the itinerant hunters of a million years ago, the more localised communities of two or three thousand years BC, and cave-dwellers of the Roman era. Not far away is the narrow opening of Elderbush Cave, another haunt of animals and the men who hunted them. The bones found here suggest such currently unlikely creatures as the lion, hippopotamus, bison, and hyena. The cave also contained tools made from reindeer bone and flint. Ninth-century Saxon coins were discovered in a cave at the foot of Beeston Tor, a 200ft limestone bluff. This is a popular picnic spot near Weag's Bridge and the confluence of the Manifold and the Hamps, its main tributary.

The Manifold valley zigzags pleasantly down to Ilam before the river is absorbed by the Dove. Ilam (Saxon for 'at the hills') is beautifully situated among woods, hills and meadows. Though essentially a Manifold village, it is little more than half a mile from the Dove and – besides being something of a transit camp – is also a tourist resort in its own right. The Dovedale sheepdog trials, held in August on a hillside east of Ilam, were begun in 1892 and may be the oldest in England. But the most unusual thing about Ilam is that it serves as an example of what can happen when a bold architect fails to distinguish bad ideas from good ones. Give the man credit for trying, but the Alpine-type cottages built in the 1830s – replacing the former estate village, which was mostly demolished – are pretentiously bizarre and out of place. They provide a jarring contrast with the unaffected simplicity of the scattered older buildings. A similar criticism could be made of the Gothic cross erected in 1840 in memory of a Mrs Watts Russell, whose family lived at Ilam Hall for generations.

Ilam Hall, rebuilt from 1826 to 1828, was partly pulled down in the 1930s but remains impressive. It is now a youth hostel leased from the National Trust (who have owned the Hall and grounds since 1934) and – be warned – incorporates one of those irresistibly tempting NT shops. The surrounding parkland is delightful. This is where the Manifold, leaking upwards as it were, bubbles back into the sunlight through a series of nooks and crannies. This is where that witty dramatist William Congreve (1670–1729), whose family lived at the Hall for a time, found a secluded recess in the shadow of a yew and there wrote much of *The Old Bachelor*, the comedy that brought him fame. This is where Dr Samuel Johnson, who often visited the Hall, derived the inspiration for the 'happy valley' in his ponderous novel *Rasselas* (1759), which he wrote in the evenings of one week in order to pay his mother's debts and her funeral expenses. And by the riverside path is the shaft of a cross – discovered in the foundations of a cottage during the demolition era – which has been associated with the struggles between Saxons and Danes and dated about 1050.

In the churchyard are two more such crosses, the taller dating from roughly 900, the Viking period, and the smaller from 100 years or so later. The church was restored in 1618 and again, more drastically, in 1884 – when the lines of the northern wall were disturbed by an octagonal mausoleum. This contains a superb piece of sculpture (by Sir Francis Chantry, a Sheffield man) representing David Pike Watts on his deathbed, attended by his daughter and her children. South of the chancel, and dating from the earlier restoration, is the chapel of St Bertram or Bertelin. Supposedly a son of one of the kings of Mercia in the seventh or eighth century, he travelled in Ireland and there met and married a princess. He brought her back to England and a child was born while they were sheltering in a forest on the way home. Bertram went for help and in his absence both mother and child were killed by wolves – whereupon the distraught father became a hermit, renouncing his heritage in favour of meditation and prayer. His example converted many pagans to Christianity and in the Middle Ages his shrine was the scene of seemingly miraculous cures. Whether all this is legend or fact is debatable – doubtless the truth has been bent a bit. But the story is so neat and touching that it invites belief.

There is a more secure traditional explanation for the faded paper wreaths and gloves hanging over the entrance to St Bertram's Chapel. It used to be a custom (restricted to the Peak District) that when a betrothed girl died before marriage, 'maidens' garlands' or 'crowns' were carried at the funeral procession – or put on the coffin – and later hung in the church. Such garlands are particularly associated with the church at Ashford in the Water. Those at Ilam form part of a concentration of evidence that the church is a substantial survival from a medieval settlement abandoned when the parkland was created.

In the area of Musden Low, with its Bronze Age burial mounds, there are strong hints of an Anglian community. Nowadays Blore is a remote hamlet amounting to little more than a church and a sixteenth-century farmhouse that was formerly the Hall. To the south-west, across the A523, is the grassy, 1,217ft ridge of the Weaver Hills, the southern extremity of the Peak District.

The chief topographical features of this south-western corner are the river Hamps and Morridge (a condensed version of 'moor ridge' or 'moor edge'). The Hamps is even more eccentric than the Manifold. It has a similar tendency to sink out of sight when in the presence of limestone, between Waterhouses and Beeston Tor. But its special feature is a course that basically runs south, then east, then north, as if having a good look round. With just a little more effort the Hamps could have transferred a large and lofty chunk of limestone into an island. Its upper reaches pass the windy village of Onecote, which has nothing to do with thrifty painting practices. It is pronounced 'Oncut'. The church contains another example of a pulpit with a tester, or canopy.

The Hamps runs down the eastern flank of Morridge, which stretches for ten miles from south of Onecote to the A53 about a mile short of Flash. Morridge is like a large book end and for much of its extent does in fact form the boundary of the national park. It is a wild, rocky land of cotton grass, heather and bilberries. The views are wide and the escarpment is used for gliding and hang gliding.

There is a road along Morridge and south of Merryton Low (1,603ft) is the 400-year-old Mermaid Inn, one of the highest in England. Half a mile to the north is Blake Mere, a pool in a dip. Legend suggests that at midnight, when the moon is full, a mermaid may bob up and comb her hair and tempt passers-by to illusory delights. Her real intention is that the curious should be permanently submerged. If the mermaid does not show up, travellers may, as an alternative, look around for ghosts (the A53, a mile and a half to the west, was originally a Roman road).

Anybody who goes anywhere near Blake Mere at midnight is daft enough to believe anything – especially if they have exceeded the bounds of discretion while wining and dining in the wildly isolated environment of the Mermaid.

2
Wallabies and Outlaws

FROM THE ROACHES TO AXE EDGE, THE GOYT VALLEY,
HAYFIELD AND GLOSSOP
See map page 60

Morridge is one of many training locations used by a hang-gliding school just across the A53 at Upper Hulme, which also has a mountain rescue post and serves as a base camp for climbers interested in The Roaches, Hen Cloud, and Ramshaw Rocks. The Peak District's western extremity is a land in which plunging lanes and lovely wooded valleys carve their way through moorland watersheds. Wild wallabies roam a lonely landscape formerly notorious for coiners, highwaymen, and all kinds of outlaws. England's highest inns – except for the highest of them all – are scattered about the same area. So are the best of the Peak's inevitably limited sailing facilities. Commercially, the Cheshire salt trade peppered the southern Pennines with evocative place and street names based on the word 'salter'.

Though it is within twenty miles of the M6, the inverted triangle formed by Macclesfield, Buxton and Leek remains a relatively unfashionable rural playground most closely associated with tourists from Cheshire and Staffordshire. Its western flank was the scene of a nine-day wonder in 1745, when Bonnie Prince Charlie and his rebel army made what turned out to be a return trip from Manchester – earning a less than rapturous reception from the citizens of Macclesfield, Leek, Ashbourne, and Derby before retreating over the same route. The Scots were not the most diplomatic of invading armies. They plundered Macclesfield for two days. Macclesfield later produced a rebel of its own, a large man called William Buckley. He was among a group of soldiers

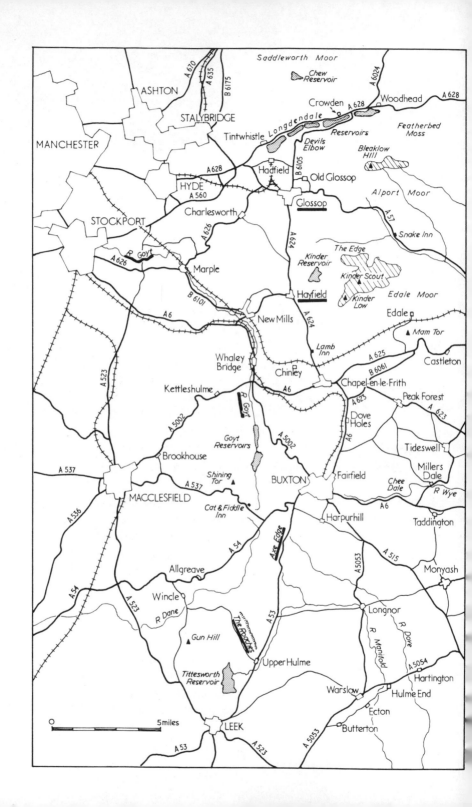

who mutinied at Gibraltar and sought to kill the commanding officer, subsequently the father of Queen Victoria. The ring-leaders were shot, Buckley was transported. In 1803 he landed at what is now Melbourne, whereupon he escaped into the bush, lived with aborigines for thirty-two years, and almost forgot his own language. Eventually pardoned, he died in Hobart at the age of 76.

There are Viking crosses in West Park at Macclesfield, and the church has a cluster of Tudor monuments. Maccles-field has been a market town since 1261 but has twice been more or less rebuilt. It has retained a role in the textile business, a role assumed in the eighteenth century when the town became England's chief silk-weaving centre and also acquired interests in the cotton and copper industries. The Macclesfield Canal, still used by pleasure craft, was opened in 1831 as a trading link with the Peak Forest Canal, which it joins at Marple.

King John's reign was important for Leek, because be-tween 1208 and 1214 the town acquired a charter for markets and fairs, borough status, and a Cistercian monastery – Dieulacres Abbey, which was to have a big influence on Leek's development until the Dissolution more than 300 years later. At the end of the seventeenth century Huguenot immigrants helped to establish a silk-weaving and dyeing industry that was later adapted to produce man-made fibres. It was at Leek that the canal engineer, James Brindley, began his own business in 1742. The restored Brindley corn mill beside the Macclesfield road is a memorial to the Industrial Revolution – and to the most remarkable man born in the Peak District.

The church of St Edward the Confessor, a rare dedication, has crosses and 'wheel' windows to remind us of the Middle Ages. The old cobbled market place is still there, too. With its chimneys and mills and dark stonework, Leek is one of the most southerly of 'northern' towns. It blends industry with the farming commerce appropriate to its rural environment. Leek is the administrative centre of the Staffordshire Moorlands District and its Information Centre, at 18 St Edward Street, is a useful source of introductory data about the south-western corner of the Peak District.

North-west of Leek is the village of Rudyard and the reservoir of the same name. Designed by Brindley, this reservoir was completed in 1797 and is probably the oldest of its size in England. There is a two-mile stretch of water with angling and sailing amid steeply wooded banks. An architect and illustrator from Stoke used to visit this pleasant spot with his girl friend. They became engaged there – and embodied the name in a son born to them in Bombay in 1865. The son was the short-story writer and poet, Rudyard Kipling. An adjacent objective for excursionists and climbers is The Cloud, a 1,126ft viewpoint that has on its flank a neolithic tomb called the Bridestones. On the Leek–Macclesfield road, at Rushton Spencer, is a church incorporating an unusual amount of timber-work and fittings that seem domestic rather than ecclesiastic.

Lapping against the national park boundary and almost surrounded by brooding moorland are the waters of another anglers' haunt, Tittesworth Reservoir, which was created for the benefit of mill-owners but manages to look natural. The sight of it provides spiritually cooling refreshment for those who have sweated and strained up the crags to the north-east.

The best known of these are The Roaches (one of many variants of the French *roche* or *rocher*, which both refer to rocks). They rise to 1,547ft. Below the main edge are pine woods and a lower wall of rock called Five Clouds, presumably because gullies draining the shelf above have split the face into five sections. If we include the 1,240ft Hen Cloud – the dramatically isolated southern extension of The Roaches – this bulky gritstone ridge stretches for a mile and a half. And Hen Cloud is only the cornerstone of two converging walls. The other, to the north-east, is that of the grotesquely jagged Ramshaw Rocks, which beetle over the A53 and were therefore familiar to Roman troops who marched along the earlier road.

This V-shaped series of edges is a fine sight. Make a mental adjustment of scale and it is easy to imagine yourself on the foothills of the Bernese Oberland. To traverse the entire ridge is an exhilarating scramble: and if you know what is what in the way of exercise and are young enough to do something about it, the climbing challenges are formidable. When the Swythamley estate was broken up and sold, sheep farming was introduced on The Roaches and for three years Canute-like efforts were made to discourage ramblers and climbers. The dispute between farming and 'amenity' interests was familiar. It simmered until Christmas, 1979, when the Peak Park Planning Board raised £185,000 to buy almost 1,000 precious acres. Times have changed, though. My brother and I were up there on a still, sunny afternoon that quivered with the concentrated care of young climbers. They wore crash helmets, denims, and tennis shoes. Clanking hardware dangled from their belts. Prejudiced by the conventions of our own generation, we used to frown on all that stuff as somehow unmanly.

To the north, in a shallow basin, is Goldsitch Moss, a morass with an abundance of pools and bog asphodel – and the shafts of small mines where a modest yield of coal used to be hacked from thin seams and distributed locally. Black Brook tumbles from Goldsitch Moss to join the Dane near Gradbach, which offers the best approach to the secluded, easily missed curiosity known as Lud's Church. There is nothing spectacular about this: it is merely a tree-veiled chasm between mossy walls of rock on an abrupt, wooded hillside. The interesting thing about Lud's Church, other than its indication of a landslip, is that it was used for secret worship by the Lollards (possibly a corruption of a Dutch word for people muttering prayers). They were followers of the religious reformer, John Wycliff, and they were cruelly persecuted in the reign of Richard II. The word 'Lud' may come from Walter de Ludank, who conducted services in this gloomy cleft in the fourteenth century.

It has also been suggested that Lud's Church is the legendary Green Chapel where Sir Gawain fought the Green Knight in a return match after their earlier fracas at Camelot. The Green Knight's castle has been speculatively identified as a medieval hunting lodge that stood on the site now occupied by Swythamley Hall, little more than a mile from Lud's Church.

Though it may seem almost as fanciful as the story of Sir Gawain, Swythamley Hall was to become the source of the Peak District's wild wallabies. The Brocklehurst family, who owned the Hall and its deer park and most of the adjacent moorland, had a private zoo. Wallabies became a familiar sight on Hen Cloud. At the beginning of the Second World War it became impossible to maintain adequate fencing. Three yaks burst through, closely followed by five wallabies, and scattered across The Roaches and the Dane valley. Two of the yaks failed to survive their first winter of freedom but the third almost survived the war. The wallabies did even better. Thriving on a diet of heather, bilberries, grass, scrub, and young bracken, they began to breed and spread across the western moors in increasing numbers. Many a drunk must have been sobered by the sight of them. Road accidents and hard winters were fatal hazards. But even after the long, harsh winter of 1978–79, between fifteen and twenty survivors were spotted. They included a robust, virile young stud recruited the previous August from the wild life reserve at Riber Castle, near Matlock. It had become clear that the wallabies needed reinforcing and replenishing – and the conservationists at Riber Castle had just the lad for the job.

Swythamley Park is situated amid a beautifully wooded, gorge-like stretch of the Dane. West of Danebridge, at the end of a narrow lane, is Wincle Grange, one of the oldest and loneliest farmhouses in the Peak District. It is a good example of what these remote monastic settlements must have been like. The monks built the present house in the fifteenth century to replace a grange raised on the same site 300 years earlier. Their sheep pasture extended across the tree-lined Shell Brook to the distant heights of Wincle Minn. A minn is a ridge but all I can tell you about Wincle is that it used to be spelt 'Winchul'.

The main road in this area is the A54 from Buxton to Congleton. At Allgreave a tiny Methodist church is tucked into a hairpin bend and a mile to the west is the Wild Boar Inn, the headquarters of a clay pigeon shooting club (visitors welcome – but take your own gun). A clay pigeon may be a bloodless substitute for a wild boar, but at least today's shooting is a faint echo of yesterday's vigorous hunting over the same bit of England. Farther along the same road, but less obvious, is the darkened obelisk of Cleulow Cross, one of the Peak's finest eleventh-century shafts. It stands on a mound among windswept trees, a setting in which it is easy to allow our imaginations to roam back through the centuries.

From Allgreave there is also a charming drive north through the winding, leafy lanes of Wildboarclough. There are scattered farms and cottages, a riding centre, murmurous streams, meadows yellow with buttercups. The valley has an air of snug, quiet, self-contained privacy. It softens the moorland backdrop. The Crag Inn – there is also a Crag Hall, formerly occupied by the manager of the now vanished Crag Mill – is a reminder of the old name for the hamlet now known as Wildboarclough. This spans a T-junction of minor roads but is mostly hidden among trees. Near a bridge over the brook is a pleasing row of cottages that used to house mill-workers. A brief flirtation with the textile industry did Wildboarclough no lasting harm however. Up a lane near the brown sandstone church is an impressive three-storey building with twenty front windows. This was the administrative block of

Crag Mill and then became the largest village post office in England – until 1979, when it was sold for £47,500 as a private residence.

To the west is the commanding 1,659ft bulk of Shutlingsloe, which is so neatly contoured that it might have been painted into the scenery for dramatic effect. Granted the time, the inclination, and the energy, you will find it even more rewarding to look from than it is to look at. The 'loe' is a variant of the familiar 'low', which has ironic connotations because it comes from the old word 'hlaw', meaning 'a hill or mound' (often associated with an ancient burial site). On the other side of Shutlingsloe is Macclesfield Forest. To avoid confusion we may as well take another dip into etymology to point out that a medieval forest was not exclusively woodland. The word referred to land reserved for royal hunting parties, as distinct from the privately owned equivalent, a chase.

Macclesfield Forest used to stretch from Marple in the north to Bosley in the south: almost fifteen miles as the crow supposedly flies. But this immense fourteenth-century wilderness was gradually tamed and diminished. Isolated sheep farms and settlements were established. Walls reached across the land. Macclesfield Forest is now a hamlet in a high-altitude marriage of moorland and pine woods embellished by attractive little reservoirs. The small, simple, barn-like chapel was built in 1673 and rebuilt in 1834. At 1,200ft it is one of the highest in England. It is also the only one in the national park that still has a rush-bearing festival. Many churches used to have earthen floors strewn with rushes or hay. This primitive carpeting was replaced every summer.

The district is dotted with extraordinary place-names. For example, on one side of Macclesfield Forest is Tegg's Nose, a popular country park and viewpoint, and on the other – overlooking the chapel – is Toot Hill. On an exposed location at 1,285ft, the latter has an oddly shaped earthwork in which the foundations of a modest building were discovered. Guesswork has covered the Bronze Age, the Iron Age, the Romans, and a medieval hunting lodge. Perhaps the site was used for different purposes at different periods. Nearby, at the head of Wildboarclough, the settlement of Bottom-of-the-Oven probably derived its name from oven-wood, an ancient word for brushwood useful only as fuel.

The Macclesfield–Buxton road dodges along bleak moorland between 1,000ft and 1,700ft for almost its entire course, and is no place to be when there is snow about. Before crossing it, let us move south-east: back to the Dane at that remote, alluring, once notorious junction of two rivers and three counties, Three Shire Heads. This is not easy for strangers to find, so put your spirit of enterprise into top gear and take care. My brother and I knew it only by reputation, and as we tried to close in by car I examined the map closely . . .

'Next left. About half a mile. It'll be all right. A yellow road.'

'That'll mek a change.'

A mile and a quarter north-west of Flash is a dell where two streams, one of them the infant Dane, tumble under little bridges. This is Three Shire Heads. The hollow is hemmed in by bracken-clad slopes, heather, rocks, dry-stone walls, and a few trees. What a restfully rich range of colour there can be in browns and greys and greens. The place is so wildly intimate, so tucked away from the world, that it would be no surprise to find Lorna Doone and John Ridd chatting by the water's edge. The rest of the Doones would not be out of place, either, for this was outlaw country centuries before Jesse James was even born.

Three Shire Heads is difficult to locate because these lonely upper reaches of the Dane lie in a rumpled, twisted, confusing network of hills and valleys, moorland and meadows, with altitude variations of 600ft. Many of the isolated farms are deserted. Some are of the longhouse type, with accommodation for the family at one end and the livestock at the other. The rough tracks were familiar to packhorses.

67

In such an undulating maze it was easy for outlaws to vanish and elude pursuit: and at Three Shire Heads they had a choice between Derbyshire, Cheshire and Staffordshire, whose police were restricted to their own patches. So highwaymen, coiners, and law-breakers of all kinds flitted across the landscape down to Three Shire Heads. Constables and men-at-arms could seldom lay hands on them.

Not far downstream the Dane gushes between projecting rocks and falls into a spoon-shaped pool. The name Pannier Pool is a reminder of the bags slung on each side of packhorses. This was the boisterously excited scene of prizefights and cock-fights (and eventually, it is said, a few hangings). Now the secluded glen is beautifully soundless except for the chuckling water and the plaintive cries of weaving, dipping curlews.

In addition to its infamous transients, this conveniently obscure highland provided a home for pedestrian hawkers who sold buttons made at Macclesfield. These shady, barbarous characters had brutal pastimes and a dialect that was all their own. They lived rough, squatting on the moorland commons. If they had a conventional base it was Flash, a favourite haunt of coiners. The local rogues were known as 'Flash men' and this became a neologism for 'thieves'. The reputation of the village acquired wider currency through 'Flash money' (forged), which circulated throughout England, 'Flashy' (not as good as it looked), and almost anything else that was fraudulently spurious. Local magistrates finally sorted out the 'Flash men'. Many left the district, but some stayed and settled down to farm work.

'They were our ancestors', joked a man in the New Inn at Flash – which at 1,518ft claims to be the highest village in England (with, consequently, the highest village pub). With a church, an inn, and a post office, Flash is certainly a village rather than a hamlet. While we digested beer and toasted sandwiches, our companion speculated about the techniques used by the coiners and reminded us how easy

(*above*) The quaint old inn at England's highest village, Flash, which gave its name to 'Flash' money because coiners used the village as a base; (*below*) the imposing façade of the former administrative block of Crag Mill, Wildboarclough, which later became the largest village post office in England

(*above*) On top of the Roaches, with Hen Cloud in the distance to the right of the author. This is familiar terrain to the Peak District's wild wallabies; (*below*) sheep exploring the romantic ruins of Errwood Hall, from which the colourful Grimshaw family ruled their Goyt Valley 'empire' in the 19th century

it was for stagecoach robbers (working on what is now the
A53) to escape among the moorland hills. At the other end
of the bar two men were talking quietly. When one left, his
interlocutor turned to us and shook his head:

'Wish he'd put his teeth in sometimes. Can never understand a word he ses. I keep saying "Yes" and "No" and
hope it's in the right places.'

To the north the swelling, desolate watershed of Axe
Edge Moor, which rises to 1,807ft, is chiefly remarkable for
its views and its versatility in spawning rivers and high-
altitude inns. Hereabouts are the sources of the Dove,
Manifold and Wye, which all flow east to join the Trent and
the North Sea, and the Dane and Goyt, which initially go
south and north respectively but both find their way west to
the Mersey and the Irish Sea. Axe Edge Moor, in short, is a
wasteland that sires a scattered and luxuriant beauty.

The highest pub in England, at 1,725ft, is the Tan Hill Inn
east of Kirkby Stephen, farther north on the Pennines.
Number two on the list, at 1,690ft, is the lonely Cat and
Fiddle, at the head of the Goyt Valley on that bleak moorland road from Buxton to Macclesfield, the A537. Originally
built to serve the older turnpike road, the Cat and Fiddle
has an unusual name that was probably based on a photograph – a cat with a violin – given to the landlord by the Duke
of Devonshire in 1857. Bunched behind Tan Hill and the
Cat and Fiddle, in terms of altitude, are four inns (all over
1,500ft) on or near the A53 as it traverses Axe Edge Moor and
Morridge: the Traveller's Rest at Flash Bar, near the sources
of the Dove and Manifold; the Royal Cottage three miles
south; the New Inn at Flash; and the Mermaid on Merryton
Low.

North-west of all these liquid resources, as if forming a
containing wall at the extremity of the Peak District, is the
long ridge of Kerridge Hill. This offers diverse views because
of its uncommon situation between an urban plain and a
moorland wilderness. White Nancy, on a hilltop at its

northern end, is a stone memorial to the Battle of Waterloo. Beyond the cotton town of Bollington and the viewpoint of Nab Head is the quaintly named village of Pott Shrigley, which is almost surrounded by hills. East of Kerridge Hill – and something of a showplace for the roofing slabs hewn from its gritstone quarries – is the attractively located upland village of Rainow. In the eighteenth century Rainow had a custom (later given a revised, more dignified form) that a new mayor should ride a donkey through the village, the mayor sitting backwards so that he might learn the importance of balanced judgements.

From Rainow a road rises north of Lamaload Reservoir and its picnic site to that strange structure, Jenkin Chapel, properly known as St John's Church, Saltersford. The odd thing about Jenkin Chapel, which is secluded among a plot of trees in an otherwise empty landscape, is that its builders either had a sense of fun or a stubborn preference for farmhouse architecture – perhaps both. The windows, the chimney, the tower's cottage-type doorway, the two-storey interior: all seem ecclesiastically inappropriate. This charming piece of eccentricity is still used for worship. The pews, pulpit and lectern are those installed when the church was consecrated in 1733. The tower was added in 1755. Beside the road climbing steeply east from Jenkin Chapel, I came across a more modern puzzle: two seemingly abandoned lorries laden with wrecked cars, the jetsam of civilisation cast carelessly upon a bare, soundless land where nothing stirred except at the bidding of the breeze.

Higher up, a T-junction of minor roads commands a choice of fine views. A ridge runs south to the 1,834ft Shining Tor along a mucky peat bog, from which Todd Brook flows north through rugged country until it is imprisoned in a reservoir – embellished by dinghies – near Whaley Bridge. The valley of the Todd strongly hints at moraine deposited during the Ice Age. Kettleshulme, 900ft up but tucked into a pleasant hollow among hills, probably took its name from a

Viking settler called Ketil. Until 1937 the village had one of England's few candlewick mills.

A minor road from Kettleshulme ascends south-east to Windgather Rocks. As jaggedly airy as the name suggests, these provide a sound basic education in the craft of gritstone climbing. Indeed, we are beginning – or resuming – our education in the special ambience of gritstone moors as a whole. In terms of wild life and vegetation, the theme is limited but robust. This is the land of the grouse, the kestrel, the crow; the rabbit, the fox, and (near dry-stone walls) the stoat and the weasel. It is a land clothed with peat, coarse grass, bracken, and such shrubs as heather, bilberry, and crowberry. There are visually refreshing patches of woodland and lively, musical streams. But the general impression is of a timeless, enduring grandeur rather than a dainty, cosmetic prettiness.

The Goyt Valley is exceptional in that it wraps all these qualities together in one attractive package: the grandeur, plus the prettiness. It is a typical gritstone valley: wildly alluring, dramatic. But it has been granted aesthetic variety by its heavily wooded western slopes, two reservoirs, and the colourful, gentle animation of sailing craft. Nor can we over-look its arresting name, a dialectal descendant of two old words (one English, one Welsh) which both referred to water-courses.

The Goyt rises between Whetstone Ridge and the Cat and Fiddle. Goyt's Bridge was a hamlet, now drowned, huddled around a packhorse bridge once familiar to the tax-dodging smugglers of Cheshire salt. When the Errwood Reservoir was created in 1967 (thirty years after its northern neighbour, the Fernilee Reservoir) the bridge was dismantled and moved a mile upstream. Its present location is near a quarry where, ridiculous though it may seem, the Pickford's removal company was born. That quarry was first worked by Thomas Pickford in 1670. He was in the road-mending business and used teams of forty to fifty packhorses to carry gritstone

73

paving slabs to London. The panniers emptied, Pickford arranged for his packhorses to transport other goods on the return journey. Thus the work diversified. Stone became less profitable, the removal business more so. But the pack-horse remained Pickford's symbolic trademark.

Not far from the quarry, around the stream that runs down Deep Clough, are vestiges of cottages associated with a nineteenth-century factory where barytes (for use in making paint) were crushed and bagged before being loaded onto the CHPR. The railway plunged into the Goyt Valley from the south-east, hit bottom at Bunsal Cob (east of the dam between the reservoirs) and ran along the eastern side of what is now Fernilee Reservoir. The present stretch of road from Bunsal Cob up to Goyt's Lane follows the line of the CHPR's steepest gradient, the 1 in 7 Bunsal Incline. Near Goyt's Lane car park is a small reservoir. This supplied water for a stationary steam engine that hauled trains up the slope. Underneath the old Bunsal Incline is a short tunnel and the remnants of another section of railway track, now a pathway. These were used for experimental purposes.

Fernilee Reservoir submerged the site of the Chilworth gunpowder factory, which is reputed to have provided gun-powder for use against the Spanish Armada in 1588. The dangers inherent in such a business were demonstrated in August, 1909, when an explosion killed one man and inflicted injuries from which two others died soon afterwards.

The Goyt Valley also had little coal mines (east of Derby-shire Bridge on Goyt's Moss), though the poor yield was suitable only for local domestic use. But the valley was predominantly a farming community (as it had been since two or three thousand years BC) until the reservoirs were made. It once had about fifteen farms. These were chiefly concerned with sheep and the valley gave its name to the Dale o' Goyt breed now better known as Derbyshire Grit-stones.

The most romantic evidence of the days when the Goyt

Valley was a working community, rather than a spectacularly beautiful tourist trap, can be reached via a nature trail from a picnic site at the south-western end of Errwood Reservoir. The ruins of Errwood Hall are a haunting, evocative memorial to a Roman Catholic family who dominated the valley in the nineteenth century. The Hall was built for Samuel Grimshaw in 1830. By 1938, after the completion of Fernilee Reservoir, the place was already a crumbling but still splendid chunk of Victoriana. So the Grimshaws and Errwood Hall do not go back far and did not last long. Their era was like a sudden blaze of light, extinguished as swiftly as it had been ignited. But the Goyt Valley was their empire – and they brought to it a colourful and exciting vitality. Their style of high living was alien, somewhat bizarre, and at times almost frenzied in its pace and intensity. They lived in luxury, entertained on a grand scale (especially in the grouse-shooting season), and had a large staff of foreign servants. The estate had its own coal mine and the Grimshaws owned an ocean-going yacht, whose captain was buried in the family graveyard up the hill behind the Hall.

The children of Errwood Hall were educated by Mrs Grimshaw's personal companion, a Spanish aristocrat called Dolores de Bergrin, who inspired so much affection that when she died in her forties a little wayside shrine was built in her memory. This touching, exotic structure stands high on bleak moorland beside the minor road that descends from the A5002 and Long Hill towards Bunsal Cob. Many a traveller in that lonely spot must have been startled yet comforted by the sight of that sturdy stone shrine etched against the sky. Fresh flowers are still laid on the tiny altar inside.

The substantial ruins of Errwood Hall stand on a grassy terrace among banks of rhododendrons in a delightfully wooded glen enlivened by a lively little stream. There is an air of beautiful secrecy about the place. Sheep graze among memories and tumbled stonework. The imagination can easily build on a ground-floor plan extending from a row of arched, sightless windows to the stables and yard. It is no effort at all to sense the bustle of activity, smell the cooking, and hear the children's voices – and carriage wheels crunching on the gravel. The ghosts of Errwood Hall are vibrantly young.

The Goyt Valley, in fact, has a lot going for it – the rugged moorland of the tumbling stream's upper reaches; the patches of natural woodland among the stately conifers planted since 1963; the sailing, angling, and swooping water birds that enliven the visual appeal of the reservoirs; a social and industrial history as diverse as the scenery; and the sadly romantic remnants of Errwood Hall. At times the valley is now more animated than it was before the man-made flood. A lane between the barrage of Errwood Reservoir and Derby-shire Bridge became so congested with cars that in 1970, as an experiment, traffic was banned from it during summer week-ends. A mini-bus service was provided for those who could not or would not walk. The scheme worked well and still does.

At the northern end of the Goyt Valley, hidden up a cul-de-sac among woods and fields in a world of its own, appears suddenly the attractive hamlet of Taxal. It seemed to me that a black horse grazing in a field by the churchyard had the look of total contentment common to all those creatures vaguely aware that life has been good to them. Taxal has a pleasing air of privacy born of the prospect its secluded, arboreal setting commands. On the terrace outside its pub are church pews for the benefit of those who like a drink with a view.

Nor has nature been much disturbed on the high, open country to the west. Lanes wind up and down a sparsely wooded, mostly bare landscape dominated by the tired-looking green of grassy hills. Two well-known viewpoints are the 1,346ft Sponds Hill and, beside an ancient road along a ridge, the Bow Stones. These two upright stones may be surviving chunks of eleventh-century crosses which once marked the boundary of Macclesfield Forest. They stand on the edge of Lyme Park, which provides a rural retreat – and an education in social and political history – for the people of Stockport, Greater Manchester, and the nation as a whole.

The word 'lyme', formerly used to describe a section of royal forest, is a corruption of the Latin for 'limit' or 'boundary'. Until 1946 Lyme Hall and its park were owned for exactly 600 years by the same family, though their hazardous life-style did not inspire confidence in long-term survival. In 1346 Edward III granted the land to Sir Thomas Danvers, one of the heroes of Crécy. His descendants were to fight at Agincourt, Flodden, and any other battleground within reach. It seemed almost incidental that one of the family was beheaded and another was fatally wounded in a duel. Luckily for posterity they were equally active between the sheets. In 1388 Sir Thomas's daughter and heiress married Sir Piers Legh. They founded a line which was to keep the estate until the Hall and 1,323 acres were transferred to the National Trust in 1946 by Richard Legh, Lord Newton, a direct descendant of Sir Thomas.

From the sixteenth century onwards the house was repeatedly renovated and altered. It remains a grand place containing many historic treasures, among them a portrait of the Black Prince (eldest son of Edward III) which is hinged to open inwards and expose an opening between hall and drawing room; a few relics of the time Bonnie Prince Charlie passed this way; and some of the finest limewood carvings in England. On the roof is a box-like structure built as servants' quarters in the nineteenth century. There are extensive gardens, both formal and informal. The park, which rises to 1,220ft, is famous for the often belligerent red deer hunted by generations of Leghs and for the sheepdog trials held there in August. Lyme Cage is a watch tower built in the fifteenth century and later restored. Lyme Hall and the park could be considered the Peak District's western equivalent of Chatsworth.

On the northern side of Disley is Wybersley Hall, supposedly the birthplace of John Bradshaw, though the family
also had close associations with Marple Hall and Bradshaw
Hall (on the lower slopes of Eccles Pike, west of Chapel-en-le-
Frith). Born in 1602, Bradshaw was the son of a country
gentleman. He was called to the bar in 1627 and later became
steward of the manor of Glossop, then mayor of Congleton.
A stern lawyer with republican sympathies, he seemed
unlikely to make any exceptional impact on either the law or
politics – until January 1649, when a meeting he did not
attend elected him president of the court set up by Oliver
Cromwell to try Charles I on a charge of treason. This seems
to have been a tragic example of a competent but limited man
getting lumbered with a role that demanded too much of him.
Bradshaw overplayed it. Emerging as a merciless bully, he
refused to let the king speak in his own defence. The trial
was a farce and Charles was swiftly convicted and executed.
The story was to have an even nastier epilogue. In January
1660, two months after Bradshaw had been buried in Westminster Abbey, Parliament exacted a ghoulish revenge on
the regicides. The bodies of Bradshaw, Cromwell, and
Cromwell's son-in-law, Henry Ireton, were exhumed and
taken to Tyburn, where the corpses were hung. The bodies
were reburied beneath the gallows – except for the heads,
which were stuck on pikes and displayed in Westminster
Hall. It was eleven years, to the day, since Charles had been
beheaded.

Before wandering too far away from the Goyt Valley we
should note that high on its eastern flank, on the other side
of the A5002, is the White Hall Open Country Pursuits
Centre, which educates the young in a variety of outdoor
activities. It was opened in 1950 on the initiative of Jack
Longland, then director of education for Derbyshire, who
took part in the 1933 Everest expedition. Three months after
the centre opened, I went there for a climbing course. The
memories are still fresh: easy successes on the instructively

encouraging routes up Windgather Rocks, followed by a lesson in humility on the more intimidating face of Castle Naze, between White Hall and Chapel-en-le-Frith. Castle Naze is a cliff that takes its name from an Iron Age fort on the edge of the 1,454ft plateau above it. The views are striking, especially to precariously poised climbers. Combs Moss, broad moorland with gritstone edges, reaches its highest point at 1,662ft on Black Edge, overlooking the A6. Prominent in the prospect to the north is Combs Reservoir, which was created to feed the Peak Forest Canal and is now used for sailing. The village of Combs lies in a vast natural amphitheatre that has been dotted with farming settlements since the thirteenth century but remained remote until the advent of the reservoir and the railway.

It was at Combs that a travelling salesman, whose line was footwear, developed an idea that was to have a revolutionary effect on road transport. Herbert Frood noticed that carters sometimes fastened old boots on brake blocks to help them cope with steep gradients without wearing out too quickly. So he made experiments in his garden shed at Combs, invented brake linings which he called 'shoes', and in 1897 went into business in part of an old mill at Chapel-en-le-Frith. Thus was born the Ferodo company (its name a play on Frood's), whose products were swiftly and profitably adapted to the new age of automobiles. Frood had a bright idea at the right time.

An apostle of a more conventional kind was also associated with Chapel-en-le-Frith ('chapel in the forest'). William Bagshawe (1628–1702) was a non-conformist minister who became known as 'The Apostle of the Peak'. He was born seven miles to the south-east, at Litton, preached his first sermon at Wormhill in the same parish, and became vicar of Glossop. In 1662 he was among the two thousand or so nonconformist ministers ejected from their livings after the Restoration – Charles II succeeding the Cromwell era. Bagshawe withdrew to the family home at Ford Hall, hard by the A625 little more than a mile from Chapel. His was a landed family who played an important role in the Chapel community, and he could have chosen the life of a country gentleman. Instead he decided to preach under his own steam, as it were. He did this in his own house, those of friends and sympathisers, and in the wilder parts of the Peak District. Chapels were built for him and Chinley became an influential base. Several warrants were issued against Bagshawe but there was seldom any attempt to enforce them. Having founded a thriving religious movement, he died at the age of 74 and was buried in the chancel of the parish church at Chapel.

The first chapel on the site, built for the benefit of foresters and verderers, was consecrated in 1225 and dedicated to St Thomas à Becket – according to tradition, on 7th July, the fifth anniversary of the removal of St Thomas' body to a new shrine in Canterbury Cathedral. This date was widely used for medieval parish festivals, including Chapel's. The market town had a hiring fair in those days. Men paid tuppence to stand in line, waiting to be hired. Women paid a penny to assemble in what became known as Penny Hill. The church tower has a peal of six bells and the old 'shriving' bell – now known as a 'pudding' or 'pancake' bell – is still rung on Shrove Tuesday. Churchyard relics include the gravestone of a thirteenth-century forester, still in its original position, and the remnant of a tenth-century cross that was found built into a wall three miles away.

The original foresters' chapel was expanded in 1380 to assume the form it has today, though there has since been a good deal of restoration. A drama enacted within it in September 1648 had much in common with the infamous tragedy of the Black Hole of Calcutta 108 years later. During the Civil War a Scottish army under the Duke of Hamilton, supporters of Charles I, were defeated by the Roundheads at the Battle of Preston. About 1,500 prisoners were taken to Chapel, crammed into the church, and imprisoned there for sixteen days. Before their release, forty-four men died. They were buried in the churchyard, where they were soon joined by ten of their comrades who perished on the earliest stages of the weary trek back to Scotland. Hamilton was executed.

In spite of its moorland environment and a long, interesting history, Chapel is superficially drab and hardly a place to arrest casual visitors. Its most engaging section is in the vicinity of the church and the adjacent small market place, where there are stocks and an old market cross. This is the area of Chapel's medieval development, which made the older hamlet of Bowden something of a backwater. To some extent the medieval character still survives in that little bit of Chapel – and in the more natural, relatively unspoilt environment of Bowden and, nearby, Ford Hall. I say 'relatively' unspoilt because only half a mile away is one end of the Cowburn Tunnel, which bores through two miles and 182 yards of the Kinder Scout range into the tautological Vale of Edale. This Dore and Chinley line, which cuts through another chunk of moorland via the Totley Tunnel in the east, was opened in 1894 to compete with the older Sheffield–Manchester railway farther north. It earned the gratitude of generations of ramblers by making the beauties of Edale and the Hope Valley more accessible at a time when motor cars were luxuries to the urban masses who flank the Peak District.

The station had a good deal to do with the growth of Chinley. But with the 1,213ft Eccles Pike to the south and the 1,480ft Chinley Churn to the north (both within a mile of Chinley), local walkers never needed a tunnel to take them to a higher and wider view. Buxworth, along the valley to the west, was formerly Bugsworth and, earlier, Buggesworth – presumably because of medieval associations with a Peak Forest bailiff called Bugg or a man called Bugge who owned iron forges. But residents were more sensitive to persistent jokes about bugs than they were to medieval history. They made three attempts to change the name and at the third

attempt they managed it: in 1929 the parish voted to substitute 'x' for 'gs'. The snag was, of course, that this prim
striving for dignity became as big a joke as Bugsworth.

In the nineteenth century, Bugsworth, as it was then,
served as an inland port. It was a terminus for both the Peak
Forest Tramway and a branch of the Peak Forest Canal. The
tramway, which functioned from 1796 to 1926, connected
the limestone quarries of Dove Holes (a village on the A6
north of Buxton, not to be confused with the rock recesses
at the top of Dovedale) with the canal at Bugsworth. Horses
were used on the level stretches but the route was mostly
downhill. The limestone and lime were loaded onto narrow
boats at Bugsworth, transported to Dukinfield, and there
joined the Ashton-under-Lyne Canal to complete the trip
to Manchester and the Mersey. The Peak Forest Canal was
built between 1794 and 1800 to carry to the Mersey the
products of Peak District quarries and mines. Within fifty
years or so trade was suffering because of competition from
the railways, but the canal continued to carry goods until
1959. The terminal basin was just round the corner from
Bugsworth at Whaley Bridge, where cargo was transferred
to the barges from the CHPR, which rattled through the
town before completing its gallantly strenuous journey
from Cromford. The canal warehouses at Whaley Bridge are
therefore doubly interesting evidence of a vanished era in
freight transport. On a hillside just east of Whaley Bridge is
a more puzzling relic, a half-mile depression known as the
Roosdyche: perhaps glacial in origin, perhaps made by
ancient man. No one knows. Though not exactly a tourist
attraction in itself, the old textile town of Whaley Bridge thus
has unique links with the past. It is also enviably situated,
because the town is flanked by the viewpoints of Eccles
Pike and the 1,338ft Black Hill: and to the south are Todd-
brook Reservoir and the Goyt Valley.

The barges nosed their way north past New Mills – which
is like Whaley Bridge in that it sprang from the Industrial

Revolution in general and the textile business in particular and could be described as a rather dull picture in a handsome frame. Formerly a hamlet called Beard, the town acquired a new name from corn mills and a new prosperity from cotton mills. At Marple the Peak Forest and Macclesfield canals combine and, as if celebrating the union, have some fun together. In a mile and a quarter the canal drops 200ft by means of sixteen locks, which must be good practice for those who need it and very tiresome for those who do not. How gratifying it is that these old canals are still used by pleasure craft.

In terms of the Peak District we are beginning to drift a little off course. But there is a name to note before we leave the canal, the Goyt, Marple, and its eastern neighbour, Mellor (where the church has a pulpit carved from a single chunk of oak). The name is Samuel Oldknow. He was a friend and kindred spirit of Richard Arkwright and he chose the Marple–Mellor district for a bold eighteenth-century enterprise. Oldknow tried to create a self-supporting community combining industry and agriculture, and he almost succeeded. The industrial development included a mill, a factory estate, coal pits, quarrying, and lime kilns. As for farming, he had herds of dairy and beef cattle, introduced the Merino breed of sheep, and drained the pastures. He had trees planted, because he had created a need for timber, and he had a small market place built. There was a lot happening at Marple and Oldknow was involved in all of it. His work did not endure like Arkwright's Cromford and financially he was less fortunate. But there remain a few proud, isolated fragments of Samuel Oldknow's dream.

A more natural marriage between town and country occurred at Hayfield, which grew up around a calico-printing works. The place meanders up and down in a haphazard way but tends to be gloomy rather than quaint, as if preoccupied by its compromising situation between the industry to the west and Kinder Scout to the east. It lies

83

alongside the bottom of a hazardous dip in the A624. In July of 1979 a lorry carrying inflammable liquid gas overturned on that road and the seepage threatened an explosion. So Hayfield was evacuated, many of its inhabitants spending the night in a school at New Mills or in local hospitals.

In addition to the thunder of adjacent heavy traffic, Hayfield has to live with the risk of flooding. The River Sett drains much of the Kinder moorland and tumbles down through Hayfield to New Mills, where it joins the Goyt. The towns are linked by a three-mile walk, the Sett Valley Trail. Hayfield's church, on a cramped site beside the Sett, had to be rebuilt in 1818 because flooding had ruined it. In the church is a marble bust of Joseph Hague (1695–1786), a remarkable testimony to the fact that rags-to-riches and local-boy-makes-good stories are not always fictional.

Hague was born at Chunal and buried only a mile or so farther north, at Glossop, more than ninety years later. He began his working life as an itinerant boy pedlar, wandering the hills with his goods in a basket, or on his back, until he could afford a donkey with a pack saddle. He learned about trade – and about the exciting future of textiles. In 1716 Hague went to London and, consolidating his association with Lancashire and Cheshire weavers, gradually amassed a fortune by dealing in imported cotton and such fabrics as fustian. A booklet published to celebrate 200 years of the Joseph Hague Trust (1779–1979) suggests that some of his profits came from the sale of loincloths to West African tribes by English traders, in exchange for slaves who were shipped across the Atlantic. When Hague was about 80 he bought Park Hall, a mile north of Hayfield, and became a country gentleman and local benefactor. He had begun life with no educational advantages and his twelve children had all died young. Doubtless both factors influenced his first substantial act of public charity: the endowment of a school at Whitfield (Glossop), the area in which he had spent his own childhood. Carved over the doorway is a beehive, Hague's symbol for methodical hard work. In 1846 the school was given a second storey, Gothic windows, and a memorial plaque. In 1925 it was closed and converted into two flats.

If you have been attentive you will be wondering why that bust of Hague is at Hayfield rather than Glossop, where he was buried. The bust and a memorial were in fact erected against a wall of the chancel in the parish church at Glossop. Between 1826 and 1831 all such trimmings were removed while the church was rebuilt. Hague's monument was stored in a Glossop lock-up where, one night, it was vandalised by an imprisoned drunk. Nor was it restored. A man called Jack White was then living in Hague's old home at Park Hall (which had its own cock pit in those days). White was indignant – and removed the memorial to its present position at Hayfield. The pay-off line was written in 1874 when an elderly man turned up. He knew a lot about the monument and wanted to see it. It transpired that he was the drunk who had damaged it. The deed had been on his conscience during many years spent overseas and he had returned to the Peak District to find out what had happened to it.

Hayfield is renowned among ramblers as the western base for assaults on Kinder Scout. In the nineteenth century carriages were driven from Hayfield to the foot of Kinder and parked at a farmhouse, where the track ended, while the passengers tired their legs and refreshed their souls. In more recent years the luck of the draw often sent me to work for a few days at Didsbury, south of Manchester. Boots and parka always travelled with me and, granted two or three hours to spare, I followed the example of those nineteenth-century travellers by trundling down to Hayfield, parking the car, and ambling up to join the sheep and the wind on the tops. On such trips there was never quite enough time to savour the rugged grandeur of the well-known walk from Hayfield to the Snake Inn on the A57, or the alternative tramp over the hump to Edale.

The old fair at Hayfield supposedly inspired 'Come

Lasses and Lads'. The community still has fun. Sheepdog trials were revived in 1977 and every September dogs and sheep are prominent in a festival that also includes a fell race up the 1,178ft Lantern Pike, to the north-west. Beyond Lantern Pike the remote hamlet of Rowarth is tucked into the hills, with pleasant old farmhouses and manor houses scattered around it. Rowarth is popular with ramblers and climbers, many of them curious about the twin monoliths known as Robin Hood's Picking Rods. The long moorland ridge of Cown Edge commands striking views towards Kinder Scout and Bleaklow – and itself is an impressive bulk when viewed by motorists climbing out of the wooded, bracken-brown valley north of Hayfield. There may be sheep on the road, so take care.

Charlesworth, clustered beside a lane that ascends from the A626 to Coombes Edge, used to have its own market and fair. But these died with the Middle Ages and Charlesworth never fulfilled their promise of a growing stature. It was too close to the older, more firmly established Glossop, a hub of trading routes ancient and modern. The Roman road between the garrisons of Anavio (at Brough in the Hope Valley) and Melandra (strategically placed to overlook both Longdendale and Dinting Vale north-west of Glossop) passed a settlement now known as Old Glossop, which lies on the edge of the town. If you want to savour the kind of scenery familiar to those Roman soldiers, encase yourself in the bog-trotter's paraphernalia and tramp from Old Glossop up Shelf Brook to Old Woman. There you can follow the Pennine Way north to Bleaklow Head and Crowden, or south to Mill Hill and Edale (unless you prefer to go down to Hayfield). Either way, you will get your boots mucky.

Old Glossop had a market charter in 1290. In medieval times it was the heart of a huge parish, most of it high moorland. This was the village where William Bagshawe was vicar, and Joseph Hague's tomb is in the churchyard. The area around the church retains some of its old character,

Two-way traffic on the Roaches: the climber on the left works out his next move while the one on the right, roping down the easy way, tries to check an embarrassing spin

(*above*) A gloomy day at the prehistoric Nine Ladies stone circle on Stanton Moor. Legend has it that nine ladies were turned into stone for dancing on the Sabbath; (*below*) the restful loveliness of Lathkill Dale spans all the seasons. The Lathkill is one of the limestone country's 'occasional' rivers, sometimes diving underground

notably in the seventeenth-century cottages. It must have been a pleasant spot – and still is, if you can shut the rest of Glossop out of your mind.

Glossop used to be known as Howard Town. The lord of the manor was a Howard who became Duke of Norfolk in 1816. He and his successors, plus their agents and a host of speculators, transformed Howard Town from a rural estate of farming hamlets into an urbanised textile centre huddled around a market place and busy turnpikes. Glossop's proximity to the Lancashire cotton industry made it the only Peak District town of consequence to emerge from the Industrial Revolution. Give or take a few years, it all happened between 1820 and 1880. A new turnpike across the Snake Pass, crossing an earlier turnpike from Buxton to the West Riding, gave the town a solid basis of communications. There were soon more than thirty mills. The Hurst Reservoir guaranteed a water supply. The railway arrived. In 1866 Glossop became a borough, with a council dominated by mill-owners. Concentrating on the mass production of cheap fabrics for the colonies, the town remained cotton-crazy until the 1920s. By that time it had assumed importance as a gateway to the Peak District for the industrial masses bent on moorland recreation. Today's mountain rescue post would have seemed bizarre to the mill-owners of a century ago.

In Glossop's enduring marriage between industry and the countryside, industry still wears the trousers. It is a sombre place. But the sight of it is exciting if you happen to be travelling east (the A57 to Ladybower is one of the finest drives in England, though snow often closes the road). And in the immediate area are the moors, Old Glossop, Melandra, and Dinting. Glossop itself is no tourist trap: just a promise of future pleasures.

Melandra is otherwise known as Melandra Castle, Ardotalia, or Zerdotalia. There is no authentic name. Its rectangular earthworks are the site of a Roman fort, larger than

Anavio's and garrisoned by about 600 men – probably the First Cohort of Frisians, which may mean more to you than it does to me. The fort was used for only about sixty years: AD 80–140. Subsequently it was much damaged. But in 1972 the council bought it and began to restore the place, to attract visitors. Down the road, beside a station, is the Dinting Railway Centre, where a disused depot and sidings have been converted into a ten-acre site (incorporating parking and picnic facilities) for a museum of the railway era. Old steam locomotives have been maintained in working order and you can even have a ride. A more formidable relic, if less fun, is Dinting Vale's 1842 viaduct: 120ft high, with sixteen arches, it is a massive memorial to an age fast fading from memory.

3
Drunks in the Graveyard

FROM BUXTON TO LATHKILL DALE AND THE MATLOCKS
See map pages 14–15

We have been skirting around the Peak District's main tourist centres, Buxton and Matlock, which is actually an assortment of Matlocks. The Romans made Buxton a resort and it has maintained that status through changing fashions and fortunes. Its heart retains the elegant dignity on which Georgian high society insisted. By contrast the assembly of Matlocks is less coherent – and less inhibited in its attempt to attract visitors from a wider social range. Buxton is the more convenient centre for an exploration of the entire Peak District. The Matlocks are the more striking in their immediate visual attractions.

Buxton (from 'Buckstones') is the cultural capital of the Peak District. It lies at the head of the Wye valley on the boundary between limestone and gritstone country in a setting that inevitably made it a centre of communications. Buxton is in a shallow bowl but sprawls around the 1,000ft mark and has the highest market place in England. It is not, however, the highest market town (that chilly distinction belongs to Alston, at the opposite end of the Pennines in Cumbria). The paradox arises from the fact that Buxton is really two towns. Other than proximity, they have separate identities and little in common. The market place is in the older settlement. The more modern spa, with its shops, hotels, and entertainment, was developed on lower ground.

The Romans, quick to spot good locations, built a camp here (about AD 80) and probably a garrison, too. They called the settlement Aquae Arnemetiae. At the same time they were busy slapping roads across the landscape and five of these converged at Buxton. One we have not yet noted was Batham Gate, which ran from Buxton to Anavio (Brough) via Small-dale and Bradwell Moor. The local museum has relics of the Roman and earlier periods. But Roman Buxton was knocked about and buried, baths and all, during the building boom of the spa era.

The gaseous, pale blue water of Buxton's springs has always had a constant temperature of 82°F, indicating that the earth hereabouts has a remarkably reliable central heating system. In the Middle Ages the healing qualities of the springs attracted the ailing in large numbers, because in those days the chore of organising a warm bath was not just a question of popping upstairs. The remedial effects of the spring water inspired gratitude, and this was naturally directed to the source of all blessings. A chapel was built near the eight springs (all in the vicinity of what is now The Crescent) and dedicated to the patron saint of cripples, St Anne. The walls of the chapel were soon decorated by a quaint variety of suddenly redundant sticks and crutches. The trappings of superstitious idolatry provoked the disapproval of Thomas Cromwell, who was sensitive about such things because he was in the process of suppressing the monasteries on behalf of Henry VIII. About 1536, the chapel was closed (it later became derelict and was never restored), the wells sealed, and the well house dismantled. But more enlightened times were at hand. The wells were reopened and the infirm resumed their pilgrimage. Many were destitute. A very different case was that of Mary Queen of Scots, a rheumatic state prisoner in the custody of the Earl of Shrewsbury, who had several properties in and around the Peak District. One of these was the Old Hall (on the site of what is now the Old Hall Hotel) and it was there that Mary stayed during four or five physically and spiritually refreshing outings between 1573 and 1584.

After the reign of Elizabeth I fashionable society became disenchanted by Buxton's remoteness and the deficiencies of its accommodation and entertainment. But within a century or so Buxton was easier to reach because of the stage-coaches rattling briskly along improved roads. In 1780 the Duke of Devonshire, enriched by the Ecton Hill copper mines, decided to transform Buxton into another Bath. The Crescent, its classic lines modelled on those of the Royal Crescent at Bath, was completed within four years. It stands near the springs and the site of the original well – and con-sisted, 200 years ago, of three hotels plus arcaded shops and an Assembly Room. A second four-year task was the construc-tion, behind The Crescent, of the Great Stables and riding school, accommodating carriages, coachmen, grooms, and more than a hundred horses. In the middle was a circular courtyard in which the horses were exercised. In 1858 these premises were converted into what is now known as the Devonshire Royal Hospital, renowned among rheumatics, and in 1879 the courtyard was covered by a dome 164ft in diameter, which was then the largest span in the world without medial support.

Within a decade of the Duke's initiative, The Crescent and the Great Stables were finished and high society flocked back to enjoy the dignified amenities of the new Buxton. Development continued for a century. New natural baths were opened near The Crescent. The Park was built – spacious housing around a central island of calm. Then the Palace Hotel and the iron and glass Pavilion, quickly enlarged by the addition of a concert hall. The Pavilion Gardens were laid out: twenty-three acres of attractive recreational facilities on the banks of the Wye. Meanwhile, in the 1860s, railways linked Buxton with Derby and Manchester. The last piece of the jigsaw was fitted into place beside the Pavilion Gardens in 1903 when the Opera House was opened – its interior marbled and gilded, its ceiling painted by Italians.

The pleasantly compact heart of the modern spa was now

complete. But fashions changed again. After a century or so of prosperous popularity, the improvements in transport that had worked in Buxton's favour began to work against it. The more exotic resorts and spas of mainland Europe were now accessible and became the vogue. The kind of people Buxton was designed to attract were no longer so eager to go there. But Buxton is fighting back, though the rules have changed. In 1979 the restored Opera House had a gala reopening for the first Buxton Festival. That has interesting possibilities. And in spite of the fact that the baths have been closed it is still possible to swim in the naturally warm water (pumped across from the springs at The Crescent) in the pool opened in the Pavilion Gardens in 1972. Across the road from The Crescent the mineral water is sold – bottled – at the Information Centre in the old Pump Room, or can be sampled from a little pump outside.

When you have had your fill of the warm colouring and gracious dignity of the once-fashionable spa, wander uphill into the unaffected, higgledy-piggledy older Buxton. Near the bus station in the unprepossessing market place is the shaft of an old cross that once stood near the site of the Palace Hotel. Farther along the busy street – in a secluded corner at the back of The Swan's car park – is the retiring little structure of St Anne's Church, which replaced the abandoned chapel that stood by the old well. Towerlessly low-roofed, simple and snug, this is probably the oldest building in Buxton. Never mind the '1625' misleadingly carved on the porch and the font. The architecture looks earlier than that. It may be that in 1625 an older building, perhaps part of a farm, was converted for worship. In 1798 the place was in such a ruinous condition that services were transferred to the Assembly Room (now the reference library) until St John's Church was built near the Devonshire Royal Hospital in 1811. For a long time St Anne's was used as a school but in 1885 it was restored for worship. At this time it became the custom to take drunks into the churchyard and prop them up against gravestones in the hope that, when they came to, the shock might induce them to mend their ways. Among the graves is that of an eighteenth-century actor, John Kane. While on tour in Buxton he ate that poisonous plant, monk's hood, mistaking it for horse radish, and died in considerable discomfort. His headstone faces west, which is unusual. Inside the church is a Saxon font that was used as a pigs' trough until 1906. The woodwork in front of the organ was formerly part of a sideboard.

Buxton has well-dressing ceremonies in the Market Place and near the Pump Room – between The Crescent and the terraced gardens known as The Slopes (once 'St Anne's Cliff'). There is always something happening. Though the town could not reasonably be described as jolly, it is usually lively and always stimulates the curiosity.

On the outskirts are Corbar Hill and Grin Low. There are fine views from the former's 1,443ft summit, and meandering walks through Corbar Woods. The quarry that provided the sandstone for building The Crescent has been transformed from scar into beauty spot. On the northern flank of Grin Low, a fifteen-minute walk from the centre of the town, is the entrance to one of Britain's most striking 'show' caves, Poole's Cavern, which supposedly took its name from a fifteenth-century outlaw who used to hide there. More solid evidence has indicated that the place was occupied by cave-dwellers in the second and third centuries. Poole's Cavern has been a tourist attraction since the eighteenth century and has all the appropriate facilities. One of the sources of the Wye, it basically consists of an astonishing limestone chamber, 700 yards long, containing stalagtites, stalagmites (I always remember the difference by equating 'mites' with little children), and strangely shaped rocks. An adjacent country park consists of 100 acres of woodland incorporating nature trails and wide views during the ascent to Solomon's Temple, a tower standing at 1,445ft on the hilltop site of a burial mound. The name comes from a chap called Solomon

Mycock, who had the folly built in 1896 to provide work for the unemployed.

On either side of Grin Low are the old quarrying villages of Burbage and Harpur Hill. Quarrymen and their families formerly hacked gloomy but roomy homes out of the great heaps of limestone waste, but by the middle of the nineteenth century these enterprising troglodytes had all been properly housed at Burbage. Harpur Hill was to acquire a modest reputation for producing mushrooms and beer.

The Wye can be seen as a child of Goyt's Moss and Combs Moss, with Poole's Cavern serving as a maternity ward. In Buxton the river is subjected to the disciplines and restraints appropriate to the young, and is mostly unobtrusive. Down Ashwood Dale and Wye Dale it hugs the A6 as if still too diffident to insist on an independent identity. Then the Wye makes a joyous dash for freedom through the beautiful gorges of Chee Dale, Miller's Dale, and Monsal Dale before returning to the A6 and more expansive views. Now powerfully mature and gently playful, the Wye wanders amiably through Ashford in the Water and Bakewell to its confluence with the Derwent at Rowsley. A short life but a full one. The Wye spins a shining thread through some of the Peak District's most attractive scenery.

Three miles out of Buxton, south of the A6, is Deep Dale. Towards its head are caves where the vestiges of a large bear were discovered among prehistoric and Roman relics. To the east, in the angle formed by the A6 and the A5270, there may once have been a volcanic vent. Calton Hill has gradually been diminished by quarrying for dolerite, a volcanic rock used as road-metal. Near by, at almost 1,400ft, is Five Wells, a tomb of the New Stone Age that is probably the highest remnant of its type in England. This much-damaged site originally had two chambers containing pottery, flint tools, and evidence of twelve burials.

Unless their visit coincides with the annual country fair, motorists hurrying along the A6 may get the impression –

from some grim, relatively modern housing – that Taddington is a misplaced segment of outer suburbia, with a nature as
grey as its colouring. The main road by-passes the peaceful
old village. In the churchyard is the shaft of a Celtic cross.
There was a chapel here in the twelfth century, possibly
earlier, and one of the two fonts in the church dates from the
same period. Until 1939 this font stood on a stone base inside
The Star (a public house, now a private house, to the east
of the lych-gate) and was used for washing beer glasses. In
the church porch is the bowl of another medieval font, and
a stone coffin lid from the thirteenth century – a time when
one of Taddington's ministers was embarrassed by a son
who became an outlawed robber. The church, which has
unusual features in its stone lectern, piscina, and sedilia,
was rebuilt in the fourteenth century while Taddington
was prospering from lead mining. There were many more
structural adjustments between 1847 and 1939 and in one
case these had reverberating consequences. When the tower
and spire were dismantled and rebuilt in 1866, the bells
could not be hung because the tower had no flooring. So a
bell was hung on a beam in the porch and a deaf man was
given the job of whacking it with a hammer to call the faithful
to prayer. One assumes the congregation kept their distance
or plugged their ears until he put the hammer away.

Taddington as a whole is remarkable for its altitude, about
1,100ft, and its ancient linear design – which recurs at the
adjacent, similarly bleak villages of Chelmorton and Flagg.
Chelmorton, indeed, is the quintessential one-street village.
It is tucked into the side of a hill that is topped by two burial
mounds. Farm buildings are huddled along the narrow,
rising road, and behind them are walled-in strips of land:
medieval field patterns that are still intact. Road and village
end with a confrontation between inn and church (partly
Norman), though the churchyard casually wanders some
way up the hillside. There is the broken shaft of an old cross
and, in the walls and floor of the church, coffin stones. At

1,200ft Chelmorton is the highest village in Derbyshire. Saxon country. Hauntingly remote. On my last visit the brooding past swept around me like a cloud in the imagination while I sat in the car waiting for milk-heavy cows to lurch out of the way. It was dusk and in spite of the solid, comforting look of the place I had no wish to hang about. Chelmorton seemed to belong to another time, another kind of people.

Flagg sits uneasily on a high, bare landscape spattered with the spoil heaps and hazardously unobtrusive shafts of old lead mines. Hugging a wall by the filling station is a disembowelled Ford Anglia cutely replenished by earth, gravel, and rockery plants. The village is better known as the scene of occasional contests in the craft of building dry-stone walls – and, most of all, for the festive but formidable point-to-point steeplechases held at Easter (usually in foul weather). This idea supposedly originated in Ireland as a playful exercise by foxhunters, who decided it might be fun to race over a straight course to a distant steeple.

Two miles to the east, just south of Sheldon, are the best-preserved lead-mining buildings in the Peak District. The Magpie Mine, with a main shaft 728ft deep, was probably worked for 300 years. There seems to have been a curse on it since 1833, when three men in an adjacent mine were suffocated. In those days three mines disputed ownership of the same vein and when miners broke into rival workings they sometimes lit fires to smoke out the opposition. Presumably the 1833 victims did not retreat fast enough. In the next fifty years the Magpie Mine was afflicted by flood and fire in turn and work was twice suspended. The formal closure came in 1924 but mining engineers, geologists, and the like continued to explore the place and in 1946 one such party reported that they had seen a ghost. The Peak District Mines Historical Society took over the premises as a field centre in 1962 – and in the first five years of their tenancy there was a roof fall, a flood, and a fire. The curse lived on. Magpies, of course, have traditionally been associated with witchcraft, death and all things uncanny. And to all this you can add the fact that some oddly shaped rocks in the vicinity have given rise to speculation about Druids. If you enjoy tuning in to this sort of wavelength, a misty dusk might give you the best reception. Go alone. But watch where you're putting your feet.

Between the Magpie Mine and the sylvan splendour of Great Shacklow Wood (which contains the tail of the mine's drainage sough) is the reassuringly serene old village of Sheldon, which was shaken up by a nineteenth-century invasion of Cornish miners. Even Sheldon has its legend. In the seventeenth century some villagers said they had seen a duck fly into a tree and disappear – and when the tree was eventually felled and cut into planks, every plank had an imprint the size and shape of a duck . . . could this be the origin of 'duck-boards'?

Around Sheldon are tracks worn by miners' boots and hillocks marking the location of old lead rakes. The industry's regional centre – and the seat of the Barmote Court for settling disputes – was the one-time Quaker centre of Monyash (from 'many ash'). Set in a hollow, this neat and sturdy village is built round a green on which there reposes a tired, battered but still upright chunk of the old market cross. The pond is almost entirely walled-in, as if to protect drunks from dunkings while they were weaving their way home on dark nights. In addition to lead-miners there were quarrymen, because 'grey marble' (a type of limestone polished for ornamental use) was hacked out of Ricklow Quarry in a bleak valley between Monyash and Lathkill Dale. Candles and ropes were made at Monyash, too. What a busy little place it must have been. Even now the village has the air of a stage awaiting the actors, and is sometimes enlivened by markets (dating from 1340) and well-dressing festivals.

In the church, beside the organ, I noticed a hymn book

(1924 edition) that was boldly labelled in gold: 'Earl Sterndale Parish Church'. The parishioners of Earl Sterndale can
now call off the search. A very long, very old chest formerly
contained the altar plate and the priest's vestments and –
like that at Alstonefield – could only be opened in the joint
presence of the vicar and churchwardens, who each had a
key fitting separate locks. My enthusiasm for church architecture falls a long way short of fanaticism, but there is something special at Monyash: the piscina and sedilia. As you
probably know, the former is a stone bowl used for rinsing
the chalice and plate and the latter a set of seats for the celeb-
rant and his assistants. Those at Monyash are fine examples,
with a delicate corporate design. The three small stone seats
are set into the wall and tiered, with the highest alongside
the piscina, and little pillars intervening.

South of Monyash is Benty Grange. The contents of this
seventh-century burial mound included the framework of a
Saxon warrior's helmet that bore both Christian and pagan
symbols. A mile away, just east of a Roman road, is the most
renowned prehistoric site in the Peak District – Arbor Low,
a northern echo of Stonehenge and Avebury. It attracts few
tourists and was never a place for party-goers. Our ancestors
must have had a heavy sense of duty to go en masse to this
bare, windswept spot. This, as my wife put it, is a land of
high flatness. Repressing her curiosity with no apparent
effort, she stayed in the car while I walked up a rutted track
into a farmyard. For connoisseurs of farmyard smells, the
approach to Arbor Low should satisfy the most discriminat-
ing olfactory senses. A sheepdog joined me, pottering at my
heels across a muddy field past inquisitive cows, and over a
wall on the left. And as I wandered around Arbor Low in
loneliness and light rain and a bitter wind the dog stood
motionless on top of the encircling bank, its small figure
silhouetted against a still but angry sky. The song of a lark
relieved the awful silence. All around, yet distant, were
smooth, rolling fields separated by dry-stone walls. The

scene had an air of arid bleakness that suggested this was a neglected, forgotten place. The sun was setting and the experience was unusually intimate. Because although Arbor Low stands at only 1,230ft it is like the roof of the world – all sky. The sun-worship theory is easy to believe.

The henge is a circular enclosure with a bank and internal ditch, neither as steeply and clearly defined as they used to be. Their lines are broken by two entrances on opposite sides. The extraordinary and puzzling feature is that there is no evidence that the assortment of forty-odd stones within the henge were ever upright. Yet Arbor Low, dated between 2000 and 1500 BC, served ceremonial purpose for a long time. It was probably a neolithic tribal centre later used for religious rituals in the Bronze Age. The round barrow on the bank contained a chamber in which there were eating vessels, skeletal relics of a burial, and animal bones.

About 300 yards to the south-west is the large, formerly larger mound known as Gib Hill. This is the biggest round barrow in the Peak District and the burial chamber has been restored. Bones and pottery found here indicated a Bronze Age burial, though the tumulus was probably built on an earlier, neolithic barrow. There are many other tumuli in the area, notably Benty Grange and, farther south, Lean Low, End Low, and Aleck Low. Between the last two is a busy road junction. The lonely Newhaven Inn once had stabling for 100 horses. At Friden, which lies on a silica deposit, fire-bricks are made at works that absorbed an old farm; and a former CHPR goods yard has been converted into a picnic site and car park.

Lead-mine workings between Flagg and Monyash are the ultimate source of the mysteriously beautiful River Lathkill, though according to variations in rainfall the river may rise from a cave in Ricklow Dale or from a series of springs among rocks half a mile down the valley, or may remain underground for almost two more miles. Even when it does surface the Lathkill remains (like the Manifold and Hamps) one of the limestone country's 'occasional' rivers. Sometimes it is there and sometimes it is not, because it tends to dive underground for a while and then reappear.

Near its customary source is a rock that is known as Parson's Tor because in 1776 the vicar of Monyash, Robert Lomas, fell off it and was killed. Up Cales Dale, a branch of Lathkill Dale, is One Ash Grange. This was formerly a penitentiary centre for erring monks (a medieval village here was deserted when Roche Abbey took it over for sheep grazing). The farmhouse was partly rebuilt for a Quaker family in 1747 and John Bright (1811–99), the Quaker statesman and orator, spent his honeymoon here. So you can file One Ash Grange under sheep, penitence, and love.

Lathkill Dale's striking yet restful loveliness inspires much affection. Its basic, rocky format is impressive: the ancient sea bed contorted and cracked by earth movements; the scree slopes created by the pulverising erosion of water, frost, and general weathering; and the delicate dignity of the flowers and trees that clothe it. And the heart of all this is the Lathkill itself – innocently clear water, trout pools behind little weirs, just-submerged mosses, and mischievous disappearing acts. The charm of Lathkill Dale spans all the seasons. It never lets you down. On the southern bank is a nature reserve: 123 acres of ash and elm woodland and shrubs and plants, protected from such careless predators as people and sheep. At the western end, as the path emerges from the woods, is a dam that provided the power for a nineteenth-century corn mill. And at the eastern end is the genially medieval Conksbury Bridge.

But Lathkill Dale is not just a pretty face. Though the scars have healed, it was once messy with all the paraphernalia of lead mining. The tell-tale hummocks and dangerous shafts are much in evidence. Some are associated with the Lathkill Dale Mine, which was worked from 1770 to 1842 (the ruined tail of its sough is close to Bubble Springs, where the main flow of the Lathkill emerges). The better-known Mandale Mine, farther east down the river, was one of the oldest in the Peak District – busy from the thirteenth century, perhaps earlier, until 1851. The path along the northern bank of the river passes over the tail of the Mandale Sough, which was a mile long and twenty-three years in the making, and some ruined mine buildings are visible memorials of sweat and hard times. West of Over Haddon, hummocks mark the line of the once-renowned Mandale Rake (a rake was a major vein, usually almost vertical, up to 20ft wide and 500ft deep and often a mile or more long). In 1854, when the mines were closed and the Crimean War was upon us, there was a flurry of excitement in Lathkill Dale because it was thought that gold had been found in the disused workings. Speculators rushed to the scene but within two years it became clear that the find was no more than the yellow mineral, iron pyrites: 'fool's gold'.

The usual approach to Lathkill Dale is via Over Haddon, which is perched on a natural ledge below the Bronze Age tumulus on Grind Low. The 'Over' once distinguished the village from Nether Haddon, a settlement that was almost entirely depopulated when the grounds of Haddon Hall were extended in the Middle Ages. Over Haddon leapt into the headlines in 1979 when it became known (on his appointment as security co-ordinator in Northern Ireland) that this was the home of the 'spymaster', Sir Maurice Oldfield, formerly chief of Britain's secret intelligence service. Educated at Bakewell, he comes of a farming family with its roots – and branches – at Over Haddon.

Long Rake, between Arbor Low and Youlgreave, has been worked for lead and more recently for calcite and fluorspar. At Moor Lane there is a car park and picnic site and some derelict buildings that once housed miners who were also crofters. Bee Low has a Bronze Age barrow (twenty-three burials, five cremations).

The name Youlgreave – or the alternative Youlgrave, as

used on the village hall – is probably a corruption of the Saxon 'auldgroove', referring to an old mine. Miners are often known locally as 'groovers'. Built on a hill above the River Bradford, Youlgreave is unusually affable with visitors and becomes particularly popular in June, when its dressing of five wells is a remarkably good demonstration of this colourful old craft. And in July there is a carnival. At the hub of the village is an incongruous confrontation. On one side of the road is the old Co-operative Stores (now a youth hostel, though still advertising 'groceries and provisions' and 'draperies and clothing') and on the other is a huge, circular stone water tank that looks like the shaft of a well thrust to ridiculous prominence by some seismic disturbance. More painful confrontations occurred 250 years ago, when the constables' 'expense accounts' referred to the forcible recruitment of soldiers, which was often a violent business.

Youlgreave was granted a market in 1340 and became a prosperous lead-mining centre. Its church, partly twelfth century, is one of the finest in the Peak District and has a gracefully impressive tower. The interior is snug and interesting. Note, first, the twelfth-century font. Its projecting stoup, a stone basin for the holy water, rests in the mouth of that symbol of baptism, a salamander, which is lying on its back as if overcome by the weight. This curiosity was at Elton until the church there was restored in 1812. The font was ejected and put in the churchyard, but in 1833 the vicar of Youlgreave took a fancy to it and had the font installed in his garden as an ornamental rainwater tub. His successor was even smarter because he recognised the Norman rarity for what it was and had the thing cleaned up and popped in the church: whereupon the people of Elton suddenly appreciated what they had lost and tried to get it back. No deal. They have had to make do with a replica.

Other twelfth-century items are the piscina and, probably, the 17in figure of a pilgrim – complete with staff and wallet – that is carved into the northern wall opposite the font. But in terms of craftsmanship the church has nothing to surpass the biggest toy soldier you have ever seen. This is the alabaster effigy of Thomas Cokayne, who lived at Harthill Hall and died in 1488 after getting into a fight on his way to church. For some reason the effigy is only 3ft 6in long. But the lad has a sword and is encased in armour like a midget dressed to kill. Under his head is the Cokayne family crest, a cock. The oldest monument in the church, possibly twelfth century, is a recumbent stone effigy in the chancel. Supposedly Sir John Rossington, he has the casually crossed legs associated with Crusaders and looks so comfortable that the heart in his hands presumably belonged to somebody else. Round the corner is a memorial window containing glass that was taken from Ypres Cathedral after it had been extensively damaged in the First World War. Before leaving the church, let your imagination play upon the fact that the dog-whipping accounts go back to 1604. Farmers often used to take their dogs to church but any dogs who became quarrelsome were whipped off the premises.

About half a mile south of Youlgreave was the Mawstone or Mosstone Mine, which was closed in 1932 after exploding gas had killed five miners and three of the rescue party. This was a large mining area and its chief drainage channel was the Hillcarr Sough, completed in 1787 after twenty-one years of boring. It became the Peak District's longest sough, stretching four and a half miles under Stanton Moor to the Derwent in Darley Dale, where the tail is still open about a mile and a half south of Rowsley. This seems to explain the startling perversity of the River Bradford in the last century, when it temporarily disappeared and ran underground to Darley Dale instead of wandering along to Alport as usual. Bradford Dale, between Youlgreave and Middleton, is only a mile or so long and has no great reputation. But this typical limestone valley, beautifully secluded in dense woodland, is a gem of its kind. The old corn mill took its power from the river and the series of pools is a reminder of the days when the only way to put fish on the menu was to catch it locally.

Alport ('old market town') is an attractive hamlet at the confluence of two trout streams, the Bradford and the Lathkill. The bridge here was built in 1718, earlier generations having used the ford, and the surviving wheel of a corn mill has an attractive setting. Just below the confluence, tucked among trees in the side of the valley, are the ruins of a smelting mill and up on the hill is a tall chimney that provided a vent for the flues.

Below Youlgreave's other neighbour, Middleton, the ruins of a pumping station provide a good example of traditional building styles. Near by, the limestone bluff rising through the trees at the head of Bradford Dale was the scene of a Civil War tragedy. Christopher Fullwood and his daughters often used to visit that bluff from their home at Middleton. He was a royalist and raised an army of 1,000 miners. When surprised by a parliamentary force in 1643, he fled and hid in a gap between the cliff and a large boulder – but was found and shot, and died on the way to prison. His home was wrecked but the vestiges of Fullwood Hall, around a mound known as Fullwood's Castle, can still be detected in a field opposite the chapel at Middleton. That chapel, with house attached, was built in 1826 and the man responsible for it was Thomas Bateman. He and his father lived at Lomberdale Hall and were antiquarians. They used damagingly primitive methods when excavating local barrows but nevertheless assembled exciting prehistoric relics. Thomas was buried beside two yews in a roadside field, and the railed enclosure contains an appropriate memorial in the form of a Bronze Age urn. Middleton has charm and was featured in the television series 'Country Matters'. In the middle of the village is a solid-looking house that used to be an inn. After clambering out of Bradford Dale on a hot day, you may regret the conversion.

The Bradford rises at Dale End but may formerly have

had its source in Gratton Dale, now dry. Gratton and Smerrill, two of the villages evacuated when the monasteries took over, are now place-names without places.

The odyssey of the Elton font began when the church there had to be largely rebuilt because the steeple had fallen down (in 1805), possibly a consequence of subsidence in an area undermined by the search for lead. Elton lies on the limestone-gritstone boundary and there is a sharp divergence of soil types on either side of the village street. The dark old village of Winster is similarly situated and has houses and cottages incorporating both kinds of stone. Winster is built on a hillside and as one descends into it from the Miners Standard (note the pick and shovel on the sign) the resemblance to the coastal settlements of Cornwall and North Yorkshire is so striking that one expects sea noises and the smell of fish. Steep, narrow lanes straggle about in a haphazard way, the result of a one-street village bulging up the hill during the prosperous lead-mining era. The best-known building, dominating the main street, is a restored market house dating from the late seventeenth century (perhaps a bit later).

On Shrove Tuesday the Darby and Joan Club organise a pancake race. In May there is a market and fair and in June a carnival wakes week features Winster's own team of Morris dancers. Up on East Bank, so steep that you need 'a long leg and a short 'un', I made the acquaintance of George Gregory, 73 years old, who had worked in a lead mine for twelve years – driving a battery-powered locomotive – and had later spent just as long with the Morris team. The sixteen dancers, he said, were led by a 'queen' and the soldierly figure of a 'king', both of whom had to be dignified and well dressed. A 'jester' pranced around them and a 'witch' went through the motions of sweeping the road ahead with a broom. A big year for the family was 1951 (in those days Winster still had a curfew bell at eight o'clock), when George was 'queen' and his father-in-law was the 'witch'. The ritualistic Morris dance, associated with spring and May Day, is traditionally masculine in spite of the bells and other effeminate trimmings. It was originally a Moorish (thus 'Morris') military dance, imported from Spain in the fourteenth century.

Winster men used to work at the Mill Close Mine, one of the most productive lead mines in the world and the largest in the Peak District. It was 1,000ft deep and the threat of flooding was constant, the pumping costs high. It was worked for centuries but in 1938 – with no new ore-bearing area in sight, another deep shaft essential, and the price of lead falling – the mine was closed.

The mine was just north of Wensley, an attractive one-street village climbing a hillside. The name may be an adaptation of 'Woden's Ley', which suggests a pre-Christian settlement. The 'ley' that occurs in many place-names is from the Old English 'leah' and implies a clearing in a wood. The Wensley district is popular with walkers and many, whether they know it or not, follow the old 'Miners' Path' from Mill Close Mine to Wensley, then down to Wensley Dale and up the hill to by-pass Brightgate. This path was used twenty-four hours a day by miners who lived at Bonsall or in the Wirksworth district and at night their lamps flickered in the darkness over the hills. East of Wensley is Oaker Hill, where a sycamore serves as a landmark. There used to be another. They were planted by two brothers who had decided to go their separate ways and find out what the world had to say to them. Wordsworth wrote a sonnet about that. A converted farmhouse at Oaker is the studio home of Pollyanna Pickering, an artist known for her portrayal of animals in general and dogs in particular.

Elton, Winster and Wensley are so closely associated that we have looked at them in turn, roaming along the southern edge of another wide area that, similarly, should be enjoyed as a whole: Harthill and Stanton moors. The former, south-east of Youlgreave, has four main points of interest. Castle Ring is the remains of a pre-Christian camp that was probably a hill fort. Its lines are broken by farm buildings on the site of Harthill Hall, once the home of the 'toy soldier' we saw at Youlgreave. To the east is Nine Stones Circle, though only four remain – the others having been used as gateposts or broken up for road-making. This visually impressive spot has produced evidence of cremation and legends of fairies who emerge at night, when the moon is full, for music and dancing. To the south are Cratcliff Rocks, well known to climbers and passing motorists. Some way up, behind a yew, is the small cave dwelling of a fourteenth-century hermit who hacked out of the rock a seat, a niche for a lamp, and a crucifix similar in style to the figure of a pilgrim carved on the church wall at Youlgreave. Beside and above the cave are socket-like indentations which may have supported a wooden windbreak and a crude form of guttering. To the south-west, its stark silhouette thrusting above the trees on the skyline, is a mass of gritstone that has been given a bizarre outline by the erosion of the softer rocks. From a distance the two huge monoliths, tempting for climbers, look so much like the chimneys of some massive old mansion that the outcrop is known as Mock Beggar's Hall, though cartographers call it Robin Hood's Stride. Some stride. Between two walls to the south is one of many local examples of the beehive huts common in the Roman era.

Across the valley are Upper Town, a hamlet that still has its stocks, and the village of Birchover, where a museum houses the Bronze Age finds excavated from Stanton Moor by the Heathcotes, father and son, between 1927 and the 1950s. By the Druid Inn (which serves a good meal), Rowtor Rocks have nooks and crannies speculatively associated with the ancient religious practices of the Druids. These recesses should not be confused with the work of an eccentric local parson called Thomas Eyre, who died in 1717. Perhaps inspired by the hermit, he fashioned in the rocks a small study with rough seats from which he and his friends could admire the view. The name Rowtor is a corruption of 'Roos-Tor'. The dialect word 'roos' indicated a movement backwards and forwards and at the eastern end of the eighty-yard gritstone ridge is a large rocking stone which could be moved by one hand until 1799, when twenty-eight hands – those of fourteen mischievous youngsters – managed to push it off the pivot. The stone was replaced but nature's exact balance could not be restored.

Stanton Moor, an island of high ground commanding diverse views, is thickly heathered and has scattered spinneys battered by a hostile climate in an exposed location. Do not be deceived by the fact that it is little more than a mile square. My brother and I, both unfamiliar with the terrain, lost our bearings in suddenly foul weather – mist and driving rain – when up there with the dogs one day in 1979. Using the wind as an intangible compass, Don led us straight back to the car – with a burst of mock-indignation when he realised that our English Setter (who was sticking close to his heels and could not be persuaded to take the lead) was using him as a shield against the fierce, windswept rain. Lesson one: never take the weather for granted in the Peak District. Lesson two: never underrate English Setters.

Stanton Moor has been thoroughly dug over because it contained about seventy barrows – many are now covered by heather and look like natural lumps and wrinkles – from the Stone, Bronze, and Iron Ages thousands of years BC. Nowhere else in Britain was so densely packed with pre-historic jetsam and this was obviously a site of lasting religious importance to local tribes. When they felt the need to commune with their gods in high places, they went to Stanton Moor. There is, or has been, a lot more in it than meets the eye these days, the finds including human bones, a variety of eating vessels and flint tools, and even some Egyptian beads dating from about 1300 BC. The best-known surviving relic is the incongruously walled-in Nine Ladies Stone Circle, about 35ft in diameter, with an isolated 'king' stone – often associated with these circles – about thirty yards away. This was probably the scene of Bronze Age ceremonies about

1500 BC but its name is based on a legend that nine ladies and a fiddler (the 'king' stone) were turned into stone for dancing on the Sabbath, which was naughty of them.

The adjacent tower is a memorial to Earl Grey's 1832 Reform Bill, which made the parliamentary franchise more democratic. Close to the tower is the oddly shaped Cat Stone, one of several strangely isolated rocks. The Andle Stone, in bushes near the Birchover–Stanton road, is notable for a carved memorial to the Duke of Wellington and a local man who fought with him. A quarter of a mile south-east is the Cork Stone, which looks across to a hollow called Thomas's Chair, named after Thomas Eyre. The Andle and Cork Stones both have metal rungs on them to aid climbers. At the northern end of the moor is Stanton in Peak, an estate village built to serve Stanton Hall and its deer park.

Stanton Moor is on top of that remarkable tunnelling feat, the Hillcarr Sough, and looks down on the site of the Mill Close Mine and the 'Miners' Path' to Bonsall, a village steeply poised at the head of a short branch of the Griffe Grange Valley. There is evidence that Bonsall was populated about 2000 BC but that kind of history has been smothered by its more recent status as a typical lead-mining village. The land around it has the usual symptoms – hummocks and deep holes – and the usual stories have been handed down about the days when the miners, a rough lot, baited bears, bulls, and badgers as a 'sporting' diversion. Some cottages had a few acres of pasture or incorporated a workshop equipped for framework knitting: the manufacture of hosiery on machines supported by a wooden framework. Hosiers rented out the machines, provided the cotton or silk, and bought the products – which the women of Bonsall often took as far as Belper, on foot. The families of many miners worked in the mills at Cromford. Nowadays the only engaging feature of Bonsall is the middle of it: the King's Head (1677) and, in the road outside, the pillar of a market cross which is mounted on ten or thirteen steps (depending on whether your view is uphill or downhill).

The great bulk of Masson Hill separates Bonsall from the Derwent and the Matlocks. The original Matlock was gathered around the church of St Giles. This stands on a knoll by the road that climbs towards Starkholmes and Riber Hill. Just inside the church is a display cabinet containing paper garlands carried in the funeral processions of betrothed girls who died before marriage. We came across the same thing at Ilam. The custom had generally been discarded by the eighteenth century, so the garlands may be 250 years old. A tablet commemorates Adam and Grace Wolley, who lived at Riber and seem to have got on rather well together. They were married for almost seventy-six years. Adam died in 1657 at the age of 99 (run out, perhaps, when going for a quick single) and Grace in 1669 at the age of 110. This astonishing partnership makes the church's Norman font seem comparatively humdrum.

The second settlement, Matlock Bridge, grew round a fifteenth-century bridge (since widened) which became a hub of communications by the end of the eighteenth century because no fewer than five turnpike roads converged there. In Hall Leys Gardens, by the river, is a tramway shelter that formerly stood in Crown Square and served as the terminal building for a cable tramway that ran up to Wellington Street (just beyond 'Smedley's Hydro' on Matlock Bank) from 1893 to 1929. The tramway's three cars could each accommodate thirty-one people and took them up and down a gradient of 1 in $5\frac{1}{2}$. It is something of a paradox that whereas this tramway was closed in 1929 because it was losing money, the cable cars that inspired the venture in the first place are still thumping and rattling along the steep streets of San Francisco.

Between Matlock Bridge and Cromford is a thickly wooded limestone gorge about the same length as Dovedale but so much deeper, so immensely spectacular, that during the nineteenth century it became known as 'Little Switzerland' (an analogy so popular that Matlock Bath station and many local houses were built with overhanging eaves). Alongside the Derwent there was just enough room for a road and a railway, at the cost of a few topographical adjustments. Two other factors hastened the development of the resort called Matlock Bath. One was its warm springs, constant at 68°F. Nowadays these nourish wells and fish-ponds. A car park above the Fish Pond Hotel occupies the site of the original bathing structures of a spa born in 1698. In the next 100 years Matlock Bath became a small but fashionable, thriving resort. The second factor was the effect of the French Revolution and the Napoleonic Wars. Between 1792 and 1815, give or take a year or two, the upheavals on mainland Europe discouraged the wealthy from making the Grand Tour and diverted their attention to the Lake District and the Peak District. Buxton and Matlock were among the beneficiaries. In 1818 a new turnpike road from Cromford made Matlock Bath more accessible and in the next thirty years high society brought gentility and elegance to this beautifully remote spot.

All that began to change in the 1840s when the railway network was extended, first to Ambergate and then to Cromford, the Matlocks, and Rowsley. Matlock Bath was no longer exclusive. It was within reach of the masses, the day-trippers, the excursionists. Boisterous, often vulgar and rowdy, they flooded out of Matlock Bath station and were immediately accosted by spivs and touts and all the trappings of a shoddy cupidity. What used to be known as 'good society' was alienated, driven out: and Matlock Bath descended the social scale and became more of a Blackpool than a Bournemouth. In the present century the gradual erosion of class distinctions has helped Matlock Bath to recover some of its former dignity, though the occasional plague of leather-jackets (the teenage motor-cycling fraternity, en masse) is a little hard to take.

Heavy traffic on the A6, plus the prevalence of 'Bed and Breakfast' signs, impairs one's appreciation of a strikingly quaint village perched precariously on the flank of Masson Hill. The façade of Matlock Bath, its shop window, is squeezed between the road and a wall of rock. And I mean squeezed. One evening I booked in at Cromwell's Tavern and was told 'It's dark at t' back'. It was indeed. There was hardly room to drop a brick down the gap between tavern and cliff. That is the only time I have stayed at an inn from which the fire escape goes upwards – yes, upwards, via eleven steps that climb from the third floor to a track along a ledge in the rock. Two days later I was on Kinder Scout watching a waterfall which also defied convention by going upwards. That was a very confusing weekend.

Like the Opera House at Buxton, the Pavilion (1910) was Matlock Bath's last substantial development. In and around this area are a mining museum, an aquarium, a 'petrifying' well (where objects dangled in the water acquire a hard coating of lime, as if turned to stone), and a model village and railway. From August to October the Derwent is enlivened by a 'Venetian' festival featuring fireworks and illuminated boats. But the star of the show is nature itself and the most overwhelming feature of this overwhelming ravine is High Tor, a broad, 390ft limestone cliff that rises sheer from the river's eastern bank. The precipice is streaked by the dusky residue of volcanic action and the mighty bluff is an inescapably awful and slightly chilling sight. High Tor grounds are more inviting, with refreshment facilities and a picnic area, a children's playground, woodland walks, and two caves that are actually worked-out lead mines. On Masson Hill across the gorge are the Heights of Abraham – a nominal reminder of General Wolfe (his mother was a native of Marsden, farther north in the Peak District), whose victory over the French on the Plains of Abraham in 1759 secured Canada for Britain but cost him his life. The ascent is steep but there are thirty acres of wooded hillside with zigzag walks and superb views: notably from the Victoria Prospect Tower, built in 1844. There are also two 'show' caves formerly mined for lead: the Rutland Cavern (originally the Nestus Mine, which may once have been worked for silver) and the more tortuous Great Masson Cavern, otherwise known as Masson Hill Cave.

A minister at a chapel by Masson Mill had a son, born in 1851, who was to found a publishing empire remarkable for the revolutionary idea of increasing circulation figures by running competitions for prizes. The son was George Newnes, whose spirit of enterprise found a further outlet when he joined other local big noises in launching the cable tramway up Matlock Bank. By that time, 1893, the old hamlet of Matlock Bank – a scattered assembly of farm workers and framework knitters – had already been transformed by the wealth and initiative of John Smedley, who had a hosiery business at Lea a couple of miles to the south-east. In 1849 Smedley was seriously ill and took hydropathic treatment at Ben Rhydding, near Ilkley. Revitalised and impressed, he introduced similar therapy for his employees and in 1853 opened the huge, crown-topped Hydro (Derbyshire County Council offices since 1958) halfway up Matlock Bank. That made his fortune because his timing was perfect: the genteel invalids and valetudinarians were then being pushed out of Matlock Bath by the proletarian trippers and were looking for somewhere else to go. Smedley gave them what they wanted (not that he pampered them – his regime was as strict as that of modern health farms) and similar treatment centres swiftly grew up around the successful Hydro. Some of the buildings survive, though their functions have changed. For fifty years or so Matlock Bank was a fashionable resort and for fifty more the hydropathic business struggled on. A by-product of all this was one of the most singular churches in the Peak District. There was a clash of wills between Smedley, who wanted a chapel consecrated for the exclusive use of his customers, and the Bishop of Lichfield, who would have none of it. Piqued, Smedley changed teams and backed the Methodists, who soon had more chapels than they needed. The Church of England's response was All Saints, built near the Hydro in 1884. This was designed on cathedral lines in order to put the Methodists in their place but could not be completed because the money ran out. The church was abruptly abridged by the erection of a blank wall, though the wall's starkness was to some extent softened by the addition of a gallery consecrated in 1958. The result may be the shortest church of its height in England. A Burne-Jones window is a more conventional attraction.

Other than High Tor (and just east of it) the most dramatic spectacle in the Matlocks, etched on the skyline, is Riber Castle. Now in ruins, this was an ostentatious, mock-medieval mansion built to Smedley's own designs between 1862 and 1868 so that he could survey his empire from a position of elevated splendour. He died there in 1874. A delightful and admirable enterprise was created from the wreckage of Smedley's vanity when a group of zoologists bought the long-deserted castle and grounds in 1962. They wanted to do their own thing and infect others with the same enthusiasm but they also had to make the venture pay. The result was a sixty-acre fauna reserve and rare breeds' survival centre incorporating a model railway and car museum. Incongruous though it may seem in the environment of Riber Castle, this is the world's chief rallying point for the assembly and breeding of lynxes (thirty-two at the last count). And as we found out when wandering around The Roaches, the Riber Castle people also breed wallabies and will release them in the cause of conservation if numbers fall too low in the wild tribe roaming the south-western corner of the Peak District.

The Matlocks may lack Buxton's aristocratic history and architectural distinction, but they have a more sensational setting and a greater diversity of appealing features for the average family. Even your neighbourhood botanist may wax rapturous about the prevalence, around the Matlocks, of the rare Alpine penny cress. And just to the south-east is the extraordinary combined parish of Dethick, Lea, and Holloway – extraordinary not because of any superficial features, but because of its associations with Anthony Babington of Dethick, the romantic idealist whose conspiratorial bungling led Mary Queen of Scots to the block; John Smedley, whose hosiery business at Lea was the basis of a career that changed the course of Matlock Bank's history; and Florence Nightingale, the heroine of the Crimean War, whose home was at Holloway. It is astonishing that three such heavily influential personalities should all be inseparably linked with an unpretentious little parish of tumbling, wooded hills, fields and hedgerows, and steep, winding lanes. It is an isolated, self-contained area, standing apart from the world as if shyly hugging secrets.

Smedley we have discussed. Babington was exceptional only in that he was the ultimate tragic example of a gracious and charming queen's ingenuous tendency to trust the wrong men. The combination of a quixotic young dreamer and one of the all-time losers of British history could not have been anything but disastrous.

Mary's story spanned the years 1542 to 1587. Had it been fictional, the publishers might reasonably have rejected the manuscript with a recommendation that the author should consult a psychiatrist. Let us consider merely the unvarnished components. Born in Scotland, brought up in France, and executed in England, Mary was Queen of Scotland when she was only a week old. At the age of 24 this sweet-voiced monarch was forced to abdicate and after that was to enjoy only a fortnight of precarious freedom. She had been married three times, which is unusual among Roman Catholics. Her first husband died at the age of 16 and her second was strangled. Her third, who abducted and raped her before marriage, had to flee the country a month later and was locked up for eleven years before dying insane in horrifying conditions – he was covered in hair and filth – in a Danish prison. During her second marriage her loyal secretary and confidant was dragged from her presence, struggling and screaming, and stabbed more than fifty times before his butchered body was chucked down a staircase. During that same incident Mary, who was six months pregnant, had a pistol pointed at her stomach: and in escaping from the murder scene she had to endure a five-hour ride on horseback. She bore a son but never saw him after he was ten months old. Driven to despair and close to madness by a succession of vicious intrigues and bloody deeds, she was imprisoned but became accustomed to finding freedom through disguise – as a man, as a peasant woman, and finally with a short haircut when she had to close the book on Scotland and cross the Solway to England in a fishing boat at the age of 25. She had already been in captivity for eleven months and in England she remained in detention for eighteen years and nine months. It is true that she had her own entourage and household effects and was allowed to mix with distinguished families. But she was nevertheless in custody – because she had a claim to Elizabeth's throne, was a rallying point for disaffected Catholics in a Protestant country, had influential sympathisers in Spain and France, and inevitably became the focus of a variety of plots. When she was eventually beheaded at the age of 44 she received a second blow of the axe because the first was slightly off target – and we are asked to believe that her Skye terrier then emerged from her skirts and wandered in confusion between the body and the severed head. The immediate consequence of her execution was the Spanish Armada, launched the following year.

You see what I mean. If anyone invented a story like that, nobody would believe it.

What concerns us here are Mary's English 'prisons' and the plot that was the death of her. She was first detained at Carlisle and Bolton. Then the Earl of Shrewsbury had charge of her for fifteen years and seven months – at Tutbury, north of Burton upon Trent; Wingfield Manor, on a hill above the Amber; Chatsworth; Coventry; and Sheffield, the most permanent 'home' she ever had. Next she was removed from the Earl's custody and held at Chartley Hall, off the Uttoxeter–Stafford road, and Tixall, east of Stafford, before her last journey ended at Fotheringhay's state prison.

Babington (1561–86), born at Dethick, was only 9 years old when his father died. He was brought up by a wealthy Roman Catholic family and at 16 became a page to the Earl of Shrewsbury at Sheffield Castle and formed an idolatrous regard for the Earl's royal captive – almost nineteen years Babington's senior. In 1581 he was on the fringe of the abortive Rolleston Plot to release Mary from Wingfield Manor, four miles south-east of Dethick, and in 1586 the young squire of Dethick was chosen by a group of his contemporaries to lead a conspiracy. Its aim was to secure Mary's freedom, put her on the throne, and execute Elizabeth – all this coinciding with an invasion from mainland Europe and a domestic Catholic uprising. That summer Babington outlined his plans to Mary in a smuggled letter and her response was a tacit assent. Now 43, she had been prematurely aged by a harrowing life, almost half of it spent in captivity. Her beauty and graceful carriage gone, she was a stout rheumatic who wore false hair and was interested in any scheme that might effect her escape.

The letters were intercepted by the spy network directed by the secretary of state, Sir Francis Walsingham. Mary's was exactly the evidence he had been waiting for, to justify putting her on trial. Babington fled in the disguise he had used, we are told, when slipping through the security system to visit Mary in the kitchen at Wingfield Manor two years earlier – staining his skin with walnut juice and wearing the garb of a gypsy. He hid in St John's Wood, then wild, and later at Harrow. But he was caught, confessed everything under the pain of interrogation, and when still a month short of his 25th birthday was dragged through the streets of

London on a hurdle, with his fellow conspirators, and hanged and quartered at Lincoln's Inn Fields. Mary was tried, convicted, and executed five months after Babington. Thus ended the story of Mary Queen of Scots and Anthony Babington. He was, it seems, a handsome, charming, and spirited man with a quick mind; but compared with the astute Walsingham he was a child in the sophisticated craft of conspiracy.

Much of this will be familiar to children through the book and television series 'A Traveller in Time', an imaginative reconstruction written by Alison Uttley. As a child she lived a mile and a half away at Castletop Farm and often visited Dethick's Manor Farm, which incorporates the kitchen of Babington's old home (otherwise demolished in the reign of William III).

From the lane Dethick looks like a huge, dark farmstead with a church tower rising from its midst. But it is in fact a jumble of three farms hugging each other for company in a remote, forlorn setting. They seem sturdy and durable but old and tired. When I arrived they were also deserted. There was neither sight nor sound of human life. Just frail lambs, clucking poultry, birdsong, and the sound of dogs and cattle within the farm buildings. The place echoed with history but the present had nothing to say until Harold Groom of Manor Farm turned up with his dog, kindly showed me the Babington kitchen with its three fireplaces, and lent me the key of the chapel (seldom used these days). You have to pick your way through the maze of farms to a hilltop site commanding views across two valleys. Even the dead do not populate the churchyard, which was never consecrated. In the chapel everything seems miniaturised, as if designed for children. A licence for worship was issued in 1229 but there is no evidence that the chapel was completed and endowed until 1279. It was built for the private use of the Dethick family, who may have given their name to the hamlet (another theory, 'Death Oak', hints at a hanging tree).

(*above*) Chatsworth House, the palatial home of the Dukes of Devonshire.
Thomas Hobbes, the philosopher, spent half his life in the family's service;
(*below*) the churchyard in the rambling village of Beeley is renowned for its
daffodils, a distraction for passing motorists

(*above*) The graceful Sheepwash Bridge at Ashford in the Water. Sheep were driven into the Wye via the stone fold on the left; (*below*) this delightfully dramatic view of Monsal Dale, in the Wye Valley, has inspired lasting affection among generations of visitors, John Ruskin among them

They lived here for 300 years and Isobel Dethick, the sole heiress, married Thomas Babington, who had fought at Agincourt. In 1530 the chapel was restored, the walls raised, a tower added, and it is much the same now as it was then – in the days of Anthony Babington.

A mile to the south is Holloway and Florence Nightingale's old home Lea Hurst, now a private residence for the elderly. The lady who responded to the door-bell restrained her affability until she was assured that I was not 'the gentleman who telephoned to ask if we did evening meals'. The Nightingales owned Lea Hurst from 1707 until 1940. The present house, built for Florence's father in 1825, is a rambling, gritstone structure in its own grounds – a beautiful location overlooking the wooded valley of the Derwent. Until the pioneer of nursing came along, the best-known member of this old Derbyshire family was probably her great-uncle, 'Mad' Peter Nightingale, a daring horseman who rode in midnight steeplechases, gambled, drank heavily, and kept disreputable company. Miss Nightingale (1820–1910) took her name from Florence, where she was born. She was the second daughter of wealthy, cultivated parents. They owned Lea Hurst, had a second estate near Romsey in Hampshire, and also spent a lot of time in London or travelling abroad. Miss Nightingale found her cushioned social life inhibiting. She had better things to do – and personal relationships were not allowed to obstruct her iron will. During the family's travels she had seen a good deal of suffering and this aroused her interest in nursing. She began her life's work by helping the sick and poor in Holloway and in 1853 she took up nursing as a career and swiftly made her mark as an exceptional and revolutionary administrator. After that she mostly lived in London.

The year after Miss Nightingale's personal decision, it assumed momentous importance. Britain became involved in the Crimean War and in November, 1854, she arrived at Scutari (now Üsküdar) on the Bosporus with a team of nurses.

By applying the principles of sanitation and constant care she achieved a spectacular reduction in the death rate at army hospitals in Scutari and the Crimea. Surviving a severe illness in 1855, she became known as 'The Lady with the Lamp' and 'The Angel of the Crimea' and was a national heroine when she returned to England in 1856. She did not like that popular image. Shunning all the fuss – the crowds and publicity, the bands and ceremonies and presentations – she spent the night incognito at a convent in Bermondsey. Then she travelled alone by train to the attractive little backwater of Whatstandwell (named after a Walter Stonewell) and walked up the hill to Lea Hurst.

Florence Nightingale is remembered for the Crimea, for reorganising military and civilian nursing and hospital care, and for founding trained nursing as a profession for women. What is less well known is that lonely walk up the hill. And the fact that when her mother became an invalid Miss Nightingale nursed her at Lea Hurst until the mother's death in 1880 – and then stayed on because of a typhoid epidemic at Holloway. It was not until the water supply and drainage had been improved that she went back to London and wider responsibilities.

It is appropriate that the terminus of this chapter should be the straggling village of Crich, two miles down the road from Holloway: because its memorials to war victims and the tramway age are coincidental reminders of Miss Nightingale's work and the world she knew. A landmark on Crich Stand, at almost 950ft, is a 'lighthouse' tower erected in 1923 as a tribute to Sherwood Foresters killed in action. The tramway museum – incongruous in that vehicles once peculiar to cities are now a village's tourist attraction – occupies a disused quarry. Amid a reconstructed Edwardian street scene and a huddle of depots and workshops are a variety of tramcars assembled from all over Europe. They were made between 1873 and 1953, a period spanning Custer's last stand and the first ascent of Everest. Many are in working order and visitors can even have a twenty-minute ride: fun for the children while their elders remember all the exciting things that happened many yesterdays ago. Every passenger is 'a traveller in time'.

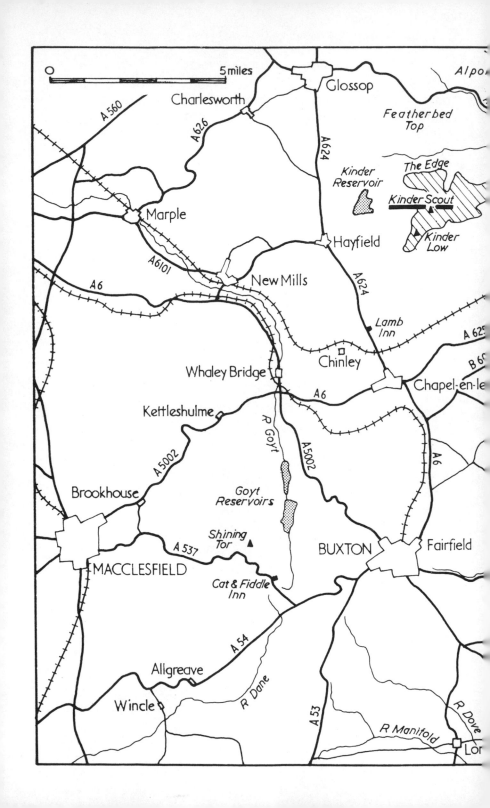

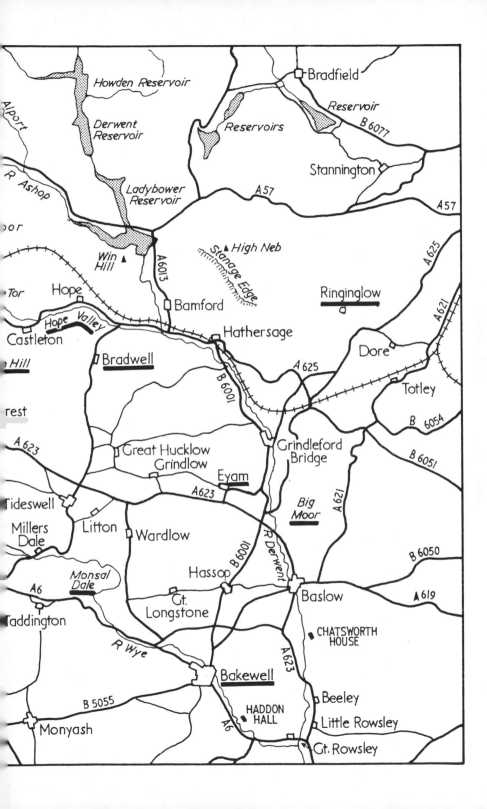

4
A Mill Called Colditz

Ashover, four miles north-east of the Matlocks, is a little off the track but cannot be ignored. Memorials to the Babingtons are more tangible here than they are at Dethick. In addition to the tomb of Thomas Babington, who led local troops at Agincourt, there is the Crispin Inn – supposedly built when the Ashover contingent returned from that St Crispin's Day battle. Less savoury but no less diverting is the story of Dorothy Matley of Ashover, who died in 1660 but was immortalised in John Bunyan's allegory *The Life and Death of Mr Badman*. According to legend she was a thief and liar who had a stunning burial. While busy with sieve and tub, washing lead-mine waste in search of goodies, she picked a lad's pocket and removed twopence. When accused, she denied the charge and unwisely added that the earth could swallow her up if she was guilty – whereupon a boulder fell on her head and drove her into the ground like a tent peg. She was found four yards down with the twopence in her pocket.

From 1925 to 1950 Ashover's lead mines and fluorspar workings were connected with iron works at Clay Cross by means of the Ashover Light Railway, which had a 2ft gauge and a 25-mph speed limit, took a big loop to the south down the Amber valley, and became popular with tourists.

To the west a relatively new name on the map is that of Matlock Forest, a huge coniferous plantation that transformed a badly drained moorland plateau. But the tree that matters hereabouts is the massive yew outside the doorway of St Helen's at Churchtown in Darley Dale. A yard or so from the ground its girth is more than 30ft. Its age, less easily measured, has been estimated at 700 to 2,000 years. So its infancy may have coincided with the end of the Crusades or the end of Boadicea, whichever you prefer to believe. Besides providing wood for making bows, yews were planted in churchyards because they were traditionally regarded as a protection against evil and a symbol of enduring life. This particular site, within a mile of Stanton Moor, has certainly had enduring religious significance – both pagan and Christian, as a variety of relics in the church and porch testify. The church was founded in the reign of Edward the Elder (899–924). But on the same spot there were Roman burials and, probably, at least one human sacrifice. There has been so much going on here for so long that St Helen's is a little spooky.

Many books on the Peak District's history and customs have been written by Crichton Porteous at his home in Two Dales. But the big man in Darley Dale – as distinct from the big tree – was the mechanical engineer and armament manufacturer, Sir Joseph Whitworth (1803–87), who was born at Stockport but spent his last fifteen years at Stancliffe Hall. He was a man of few words but his response to every mechanical problem was 'Let's try' and his entire life stressed initiative, planning and precision. He made his name and his fortune from revolutionary improvements in machinery (notably a measuring device) and from the Whitworth rifle. In Darley Dale he meticulously created an interesting estate in a difficult location and was a generous philanthropist. The Whitworth Institute was used for military purposes in both world wars.

Straddling the A6 at the confluence of the Derwent and the Wye is Rowsley, which took its name from the Rollesley family. From 1849 to 1863 a ducal deadlock made Rowsley the unexpected terminus of a railway that was intended to link Derby and Manchester, and eventually did. The Duke of Devonshire would not tolerate the line's extension via the

Derwent and Chatsworth Park. For fourteen years the Duke of Rutland was similarly obdurate about an extension via the Wye. Then he permitted tunnelling through a hillside at the back of Haddon Hall as long as no trees were damaged. Five men were killed when the tunnel collapsed during construction. Each Duke insisted on having his own station, so the Duke of Rutland was given special facilities at Bakewell and the Duke of Devonshire was granted a 'request stop' a mile south of Hassop.

The freight depot of the Rowsley station is now incorporated in the premises of an engineering firm on the north side of the A6. But Rowsley's best-known building is that attractive and genteel rendezvous for anglers, the Peacock Hotel (the peacock is the crest of the Manners family, including the Dukes of Rutland). The Peacock was built in 1652 as a manor house but became a hotel in 1828 when the village's two post inns were closed. The church has two unusual features. Poised on a window sill is the head of a ninth-century cross that was discovered by two local boys while they were swimming in the Wye. And tucked away in a corner is a framed memorial – touching in its simplicity and implications – to an airman killed on active service in 1918. In boyhood he had spent many happy holidays at Rowsley and his sunny nature had obviously endeared him to the daughters of the Duke and Duchess of Rutland.

In 1912 the same Duke of Rutland began the painstaking task of restoring Haddon Hall, a chore that took twenty years but was done well. This may be England's finest medieval mansion but its sturdy grey-brown grandeur is reassuring rather than intimidating. Haddon Hall has harmony without symmetry, dignity without affectation. In spite of the towers and turrets and battlemented walls it has always been a home rather than a castle, and in 900 years it has been owned by only four families. The first house was built for William Peveril, illegitimate son of William the Conqueror, but in 1153 that line was disinherited and the estate was granted to the tenant, William Avenil. In 1170 he divided the manor between two sons-in-law and Haddon went to the Vernon branch, who kept it until 1567. Then Sir George Vernon died without a male heir and the property went to his daughter Dorothy, whose marriage to John Manners launched a continuity of ownership that still endures. In short, Haddon Hall has been in the hands of the Vernon and Manners families for more than 800 years.

Structural adjustments and extensions were almost exclusively confined to the fourteenth, fifteenth and sixteenth centuries, when generations of Vernons had money to burn because of their profits from lead mines and estates. But in 1641 the Haddon branch of the Manners family inherited the Rutland title and went to live at another ancestral home, Belvoir Castle, near Grantham. And for almost 250 years Haddon Hall was uninhabited, unfurnished, and unchanged, though the building itself was maintained in sound condition. This period was a boon for posterity because it meant that at a time when wholesale rebuilding was fashionable, nobody messed about with Haddon Hall. That is why we see it now much as it was when the Manners took over from the Vernons in the sixteenth century, the most romantic era in the estate's history.

While Haddon Hall was unoccupied it became a legendary tourist attraction (in 1832 the visitors included the 13-year-old Princess Victoria) and we may reasonably be sceptical about the fact that in 1822 the details of Dorothy Vernon's supposed elopement with John Manners, 264 years earlier, emerged for the first time. They certainly married. But could anything so titillating as an elopement have remained a family secret for so long? The last of the Vernons, Sir George, was so immensely wealthy that he lived like a king – and so powerfully autocratic that he had his retainers hang a local murderer without trial. We are told that he played the heavy father (a role totally in character) when Dorothy took a fancy to John, second son of the Earl of Rutland. After all, the fellow was not even a knight! The story goes that during a ball Dorothy nipped out of the Long Gallery into an ante-room and down through the gardens to the Wye, where her boy friend was waiting with horses by the packhorse bridge. This tale can be challenged on points of detail but could have a basis of truth. We may never know.

Haddon Hall is renowned for its tapestries and you will doubtless visit the banqueting hall, kitchen, bakery, dining room, Great Chamber, Long Gallery, museum, and chapel. The banqueting hall has a minstrels' gallery, which is not surprising, and an iron manacle, which is. It seems that any guest who was not drinking fast enough had one wrist manacled, and the arrears of booze were then poured down his sleeve. The chapel, which has a three-decker pulpit and a series of murals, was probably the church of Nether Haddon, a village that as we already know was evacuated when the estate was extended. The Hall is delightfully located between the Wye and a wooded hill. Roses are abundant in the terraced gardens, which fall away to a stretch of the Wye well known for its trout and grayling.

North of Rowsley – and mostly just far enough away from the southern approach road to Chatsworth Park to be spared the worst of the bustle and stench – is the haphazard old village of Beeley, which has a brook running through it, a little green, a fine display of daffodils in the churchyard, and a seventeenth-century inn, the Devonshire Arms, that has been modernised but remains compatible with its context. Yet Beeley seldom gets more than an admiring glance from passing motorists. To the east, the marshy wasteland of East Moor commands views towards the night-glow of Sheffield and Chesterfield. Here a watercourse is called a 'sick'. The alternative forms 'sike' or 'sitch' often refer to ditches. Hob Hurst's House, a Bronze Age burial mound on the edge of Bunker's Hill Wood, can be readily translated if we read 'hob' as 'hobgoblin' or 'elf' and 'hurst' as 'a wooded or secluded spot'.

This was the vicinity, perhaps the very place, where a Scot called John Beaton met two conspirators at five o'clock one chilly morning, more than 400 years ago, to discuss their plans for releasing Mary Queen of Scots from Chatsworth House. The faithful Beaton was the master of Mary's household and had already helped her to escape from Lochleven Castle. The Chatsworth plot came to nothing and by the time it was discovered Beaton could not be tried because he was dead (1572). In the chancel of Edensor Church there is a brass to his memory. Mary must have had a stimulating relationship with her custodian's wife, Bess of Hardwick, more than twenty years her senior. Both were having uncommonly eventful lives and they had a combined tally of seven husbands; so there must have been plenty to talk about while they were sitting at their embroidery. Bess was popped into the Tower of London for a few months because Elizabeth I suspected her of scheming on Mary's behalf. But the Shrewsbury marriage eventually turned sour and Bess became jealous of her husband's regard for Mary. There was a nasty quarrel and Bess left her husband and Chatsworth and moved back to her birthplace, Hardwick, where she had another great house built. Because of the scandal, Mary was removed from the Earl's custody.

Bess was intelligent and fearless, witty and waspish – difficult to tolerate but difficult to resist. A squire's daughter who made a career out of marriage, money, and mansions, she had four husbands and became wealthier with every change. When her last husband – the Earl of Shrewsbury – died in 1590, she was the richest woman in England except for the Queen. Bess and her second husband, Sir William Cavendish, bought the Chatsworth estate and in 1552 began the first house on the site. They also had six children and founded the Cavendish line. Bess finished that first house after her husband's death. Nothing remains of it but in the park are two buildings that date from her time: a 'hunting tower' that was really a gazebo for spotting deer and watching the hunt, and a summer refuge known as 'Queen Mary's Bower' because it was supposedly one of Mary's favourite haunts. The first house was demolished and between 1687 and 1707 a second was built for Bess's grandson, who became the first Duke of Devonshire after he had helped William III to the throne. 'Devonshire' instead of 'Derbyshire' may have been a clerical error, never corrected because it would have been too much trouble. The sixth Duke, who acceded in 1811, made a lot of money from lead and copper mines and spent it freely on Chatsworth's house and grounds, assembling many works of art while he was about it.

Chatsworth House is magnificently palatial, inside and out. The closer you get, the more impressive and exhilarating it becomes. Wandering round the place is rather like exploring a village – sumptuously designed, decorated, and furnished – that has been built in connected pieces. The splendour of the state apartments is probably unsurpassed, in Europe anyway. Renowned artists and craftsmen were brought over from mainland Europe, each to create his own kind of beauty. But a minor Dutch painter was responsible for the teasing deception of what seems to be a violin and bow hanging on a door in the music room. And much of the wood-carving and sculpture was bequeathed to a grateful posterity by Samuel Watson of Heanor (twenty miles to the south-east), who worked at Chatsworth from 1689 to 1709. His era succeeded that of Thomas Hobbes, the philosopher best known for *The Leviathan*, who served the Cavendish family as tutor and secretary for half his life. And we should note that one of England's most famous chemists and physicists was Henry Cavendish (1731–1810), grandson of the second Duke.

There were celebrities working outdoors, too. From 1760 onwards the park and gardens were landscaped by Lancelot 'Capability' Brown, and Sir Joseph Paxton (1803–65) became head gardener at the age of 23 and challenged Hobbes and Watson in continuity of service before being buried at Edensor. The iron and glass Great Conservatory at Chatsworth, built from 1836 to 1840, was Paxton's model for the 1851 Crystal Palace. The Conservatory was pulled down in 1920 and a yew maze laid out within its foundations. Chatsworth's aquatic arrangements are spectacular: not least the Cascade, a 200-yard staircase of water, and the Emperor Fountain, which at full power can throw a jet 290ft up, the highest fountain in Europe. It was designed and named in honour of Tsar Nicholas I, who was due to visit Chatsworth but never turned up.

Either Chatsworth or Willersley Castle (near Cromford), perhaps both, is believed to have been the model for Darcy's Pemberley in *Pride and Prejudice*. The description of the landscape could fit either but the comments on the interior do not make sense in terms of Chatsworth. The novel refers to Chatsworth, Matlock, Dovedale, and Bakewell. There is no evidence that Jane Austen visited either house – nor, indeed, that she ever travelled north of the Trent. But she could easily have based her fictional detail on illustrated tourists' guides and other second-hand information, both documentary and verbal. An amusing but slightly alarming development is a legend based on the naïve assumption that because she wrote about these places she must have visited them. This assumption emerged in a 1936 guide to Bakewell (125 years after the supposed event – a suspicious parallel with the retarded publication of the Vernon–Manners elopement story). A local writer, having made descriptive comparisons and calculated guesses, embellished the theory with speculative suggestions that Miss Austen had stayed in Bakewell at the Rutland Arms in 1811 and had there revised *Pride and Prejudice*, making the hotel the setting for an emotional passage in the novel. The extraordinary thing is that this fanciful farrago is so widely accepted as the truth. The committee of the Jane Austen Society would like to believe the story but can find no foundation for it. She may or may not have visited the Peak District. No one knows.

Chatsworth took its name from Ceatt, a Saxon landowner,

the 'worth' commonly indicating it was a settlement or some spot enclosed for cultivation. The place is a four-piece wonderland: the scenery of the park, the landscaping of the gardens, the architecture of the house, and the artistry and craftsmanship of its contents. Chatsworth's annual horse trials are a feature of the Peak District's calendar. There are deer in the park, though you will be lucky to get more than a distant view of them (if that). The southern approach is via Beeley and a seventeenth-century bridge, the northern approach via Edensor (pronounced 'Ensor'), where a handsome brick building with a portico stands back from the road just outside the park gates. Now the estate office, this was built about 1775 as a genteel inn catering for stagecoach travellers and Chatsworth's fashionable visitors (Johnson and Boswell among them).

On the same side of the road, but inside the park, an isolated house with a walled garden stands in a hollow formerly occupied by a Saxon village that became the sprawling small town of Edensor. The fourth Duke of Devonshire had the lowest section of the town demolished because it spoiled his view. By 1838 the sixth Duke had cleared the rest of the hollow except for that single house, which used to be alongside the High Street of the old town. During the demolition period it had been occupied for at least fifty years by Anthony Holmes (perhaps father and son in turn). Either he owned it and refused to sell, or he was a respected elderly tenant and the Duke decided to let him die there before pulling the place down. Anyway, as the years went by the house came to be regarded as a relic to be preserved rather than an eyesore to be removed.

The people evacuated from Edensor were rehoused at Pilsley, a village created for the purpose. Pilsley is a pleasant little backwater that has a fair and a well-dressing festival and buildings that date from both periods of Edensor's destruction. Nothing survived that destruction except for the Holmes house, the inn, and a few dwellings in the existing village of Edensor across the road. The proud remnants include the 'Swiss cottage' and its neighbour overlooking the green and, behind them, the post office and adjoining cottage. While most of Edensor was being removed from the landscape, that Swiss-style structure became an alehouse for the villagers: the inn was too smart for them. Today's Edensor, the upper part of the old town, was remodelled, knocked about, and rebuilt as an estate village between 1837 and 1841. Cushioned by trees and shrubs, it has such a mellow serenity that it seems to be posing – as if it was a film set, or a model village that had outgrown the designer's conception. The architect consulted a popular pattern book and (out of a spirit of enterprise, a sense of fun, or plain indecision) used an extraordinary diversity of styles. Almost every cottage is different, but the eccentricity is pleasing because of the overall harmony. The only jarring feature is the church (rebuilt from 1866 to 1870), which seems overwhelmingly out of proportion because of its size and raised site. Those buried here include Lord Frederick Cavendish, the Irish Secretary, who was murdered in Phoenix Park, Dublin, in 1882.

The sturdy, genial, traffic-busy village of Baslow, a familiar sight to travellers and tourists, is enviably situated in a broad stretch of the Derwent valley, with Chatsworth to the south and gritstone edges to the north and east. Baslow is a four-part village. There is an old toll house at Far End, a sparse farming community on the Sheffield road. The residential area is Over End, up the hill. The bit best known to visitors is Nether End, gathered round a green, where the Devonshire Arms and Cavendish Hotel (note the symbolic snake, the Cavendish family crest) remind us where we are. Bridge End, huddled round the church by the river, is the original settlement. The main flow of traffic passes it by, over a wide modern bridge, but on the other side of the church is a charming little bridge about 500 years old. At one end, with a peephole in the wall, is a shelter that probably served as sentry post and toll house in turn. There is a royalist confrontation between the Prince of Wales inn and the dial of the church clock, which spells out 'Victoria 1897' (to mark the diamond jubilee) instead of being numbered from 1 to 12 in the usual way. The church tower and spire are thirteenth century, ancient coffin stones are built into the porch and the lintels of the clerestory windows, and just inside the doorway is a formidable dog whip (a rare relic) and a pitch-pipe that was used for tuning the organ.

Sebastian de Ferranti (1864–1930), the electrical engineer, lived for twenty-four years at Baslow and Grindleford. His professional enthusiasm spilled over into his private life and he stocked Baslow Hall with labour-saving electrical gadgets. It is said that one experiment had unfortunate consequences when he tried battery poultry farming and electrocuted the chickens.

Just along the road at Calver Bridge (pronounced 'Carver') is a structure familiar to millions who have never been near it: a former cotton mill, one of England's earliest factories, that represented Colditz Castle in the television series. Outwardly much the same as it was when completed in 1786, the mill and adjacent wheelhouse are architecturally enlightening. But there is no public access. Cotton was produced until 1923 but there was not much further use for the mill until 1947, when it was bought and internally modified by W. and G. Sissons (a company the same age as the building) for the manufacture of stainless-steel sinks and other kitchen equipment. Also at Calver Bridge is the Derbyshire Craft Centre, which has a shop, art gallery, restaurant, and children's playroom – a shrewd precautionary facility for a business specialising in pottery.

Stoney Middleton has been an industrial village for centuries: mining, boot-making, and, more recently, limestone quarrying and a huge plant for grinding fluorspar. Because of the lorry traffic and the greenery's coating of grey dust, the village is more likely to offend tourists than attract them.

In a private garden at Curbar is this old lock-up, where malefactors were detained until they could be moved to a proper jail. It was later used as a modest home until the 1930s. The conical roof, built on to an otherwise square structure, demanded intricate internal architecture. On the open moorland near by are the simple graves of five Plague victims

(*above*) Two examples of well dressing, at Hope. Moss, leaves, and flowers, pressed on to damp clay covering boards, are among the materials used in a painstaking craft that could have pagan origins; (*below left*) Little John's grave in the churchyard at Hathersage. He may have been a local nailmaker who became a soldier and outlaw. Legend says that, with death imminent, he shot an arrow from his adjacent cottage and asked to be buried where it fell – in the shade of a yew; (*below right*) a quiet, leafy corner of Edale, southern extremity of the Pennine Way. The name 'Edale' was formerly applied to the entire valley, which is almost surrounded by high moorland. The original settlements were five 'booths', farm holdings rented from the Crown by foresters or private landowners

Yet it lies in a spectacular gorge. In 1760, it is said, a girl unlucky in love leapt from Lover's Leap but struck lucky because, when picked up, she was merely bruised and shaken. There is also a cave which for years concealed the murder of an old Scottish pedlar. During the mining era the straggling one-street village spread up the steep slopes wherever it could find a perch, and once you get away from the A623 it is unexpectedly cosy. The church has an extraordinary octagonal design and stands by a brook in a secluded setting where warm springs were formerly used for hydropathic bathing. Nowadays the same spot is the scene of well dressing and Maypole dancing.

Stoney Middleton had a celebrity called Thomas Denman who kept black pigs and often took one with him as a present when visiting friends. I have not identified this chap. But a Thomas Denman born at Bakewell in 1733 went to London and became a pioneer in obstetrics – and his son, born in London in 1779, who certainly inherited an estate at Stoney Middleton and spent a lot of time there, was the Thomas Denman who became Lord Chief Justice of England.

Coombs Dale is interesting because of its flora and old ash woods, Longstone Edge because of an enclosure protecting the rare dark red helleborine, and Bleaklow because of a tumulus where skeletons were found. But half a mile from Calver on the road to Hassop, the tail of an old sough gives us a better idea what to expect from Longstone Moor and its environs – especially High Rake, which rises to almost 1,300ft. Mining and a subsequent quest for fluorspar and other minerals have made a dreadful mess up there. Longstone Edge overlooks the ancient settlement of Rowland, which has played a variety of roles in farming and mining, and the villages of Hassop and Great Longstone. Hassop has a sternly formal Roman Catholic church that looks rather at odds with its environment. Hassop Hall and its park are known chiefly for the legend of a respected 'talking' beech tree. When ownership of the Hall was in dispute, the beech supposedly made regular pronouncements to the effect that it would not shut up until the authentic heir took over the estate. Great Longstone is a typical limestone village and the Crispin Inn reminds us that mining was not the only local industry (St Crispin is the patron saint of shoemakers). The pulpit of the church has a pillar of Duke's Red Marble, limestone impregnated with iron, which was mined at Alport in the nineteenth century.

Bakewell, the national park's administrative 'capital', is renowned for its agricultural and horticultural show, its well dressings and carnivals, and its Monday markets. These markets date from 1330 but a charter for a market and fair was granted in 1254 and Bakewell must have been a busy trading centre long before that. The first half of its name is a corruption of either 'Badeca', indicating a Saxon, or 'bad' – bath or spring. There were about a dozen wells, now mostly dry or filled in, but at 60°F the water was cooler than that at Buxton and Matlock and consequently Bakewell hardly came under starter's orders as a spa. A memento is the partly rebuilt bath house erected for the Duke of Rutland in 1697. North-east of the town is Ballcross, with the rampart and ditch of a minor hill fort more than 2,000 years old. The finds there included Iron Age pottery and a primitive hand mill for grinding grain. Castle Hill has the earthworks of a small castle that probably dates from the twelfth-century wars between King Stephen and his cousin Matilda, who were disputing the throne. Edward the Elder, son of Alfred the Great, gave the Danes a hiding and pushed his father's kingdom farther north. In 924 Edward ordered that a castle should be built at Bakewell and garrisoned, but he died that year and there is no evidence that these orders were carried out. Ballcross was too early, Castle Hill probably too late.

Bakewell's origins are almost ostentatiously Saxon. The church of All Saints, on a steep site commanding wide views, has an astonishing collection of worn and battered Saxon masonry – notably coffin stones and crosses. The south porch is a miniature storeroom, there are more fragments at the west end of the church, and enough Saxon stonework to build a small house was incorporated in the walls when the original church was replaced in the twelfth century (further drastic changes have rather confused the structural pedigree). The two Saxon crosses in the churchyard both came from afar. Close to the east wall of the Vernon Chapel is a remarkable and renowned preaching cross, 8ft tall and dating from AD 750 to 800, that supposedly stood by an ancient crossroads near Hassop station. The tenth-century shaft near the south porch was dug up near Burley Fields Farm in Darley Dale.

The Vernon Chapel contains the tomb and effigy of the 'King of the Peak', Sir George Vernon, and a monument to his daughter Dorothy and John Manners, who both look so sour that the romantic story of their elopement is hard to believe. The church has a sedilia and double piscina and a font made from a single block of gritstone. Punsters who lift the seat of the priest's stall will enjoy the carving on the misericord, which depicts three rotten teeth and a cow to suggest that three 'acres' and a cow are the key to contentment. Another uncommon feature of the church is its octagonal tower and battlemented walls. And note the relatively modern lych-gate ('lych' meant 'corpse' and it was in these roofed gateways that loaded coffins awaited the minister's arrival). At the lower end of the churchyard is the grave of White Watson, sculptor, mineralogist and antiquary. Samuel Watson, whom we met at Chatsworth, was the father of White's uncle, Henry, whom we shall meet at Ashford in the Water.

Up the hill behind the church is the engagingly venerable Old House, which dates from 1534 and has been restored as a museum. 'Downtown' is the Market Hall, rebuilt in the seventeenth century and recently renovated for use as a national park information centre, and the old Town Hall

(1602), which has been adapted to serve a variety of purposes. Quarter sessions were held here until 1897 and although the old cells are no longer recognisable, their shell survives. The Rutland Arms, built in 1804 on the site of the former White Horse Inn, is a pleasant hotel with an unusual claim to our attention. The Jane Austen legend is based on nothing but speculation and wishful thinking. It is true, though, that Bakewell puddings (now generally known as tarts) were accidentally created here about 1860. One of the kitchen staff misunderstood instructions and either poured egg mixture onto strawberry jam tarts – or, instead of pouring the mixture into a pastry case and topping it with jam, put them in the other way round. Whatever the exact nature of the error, it produced a tasty extension to England's culinary traditions.

Bakewell's town bridge probably dates from the fourteenth century but has since been widened. Upstream is an old packhorse route across Holme Bridge, which was rebuilt in 1664 as a link with the hamlet gathered round Holme Hall (1626). Near by is the site of Richard Arkwright's cotton-spinning factory, Lumford Mill, built between 1778 and 1782 in spite of the Duke of Rutland's opposition. The mill employed about 300 people, mostly women and children, but was burnt down in 1868. A row of the workers' cottages is still there. This has remained the town's industrial quarter and downstream at the old Victoria corn mill, which retains its water wheel, is a somewhat idiosyncratic company which produces animal pictures and pharmaceutical goods for the pet trade.

Bakewell has not changed much since Dorothy Vernon's daughter-in-law, Lady Grace Manners, founded a distinguished school here in 1637. Unspoilt, pleasantly compact and busy, it is an agreeable place to saunter about – in the shopping area, or up the hill around the church, or on the popular riverside walk where rainbow trout accept food from trippers (the Wye is an exceptional river in that rainbow trout reproduce in it). Bakewell is a good starting point for a tour of the Peak District and no bad terminus either.

Ashford in the Water is not the leafy Venice it sounds, but fits neatly into an alluring environment. A minor castle – once in the custody of Edmund, youngest son of Edward I – has vanished without trace from a field behind the church. The village combines a well-dressing festival with Morris dancing and a sheep-shearing demonstration at the lovely Sheepwash Bridge, built in the seventeenth century at a time when as many as 300 packhorses passed this way every week, carrying malt from Derby. Note the stone fold at one end of the bridge. For centuries sheep were driven into the fold and had to take a bath because the only exit was into the river, an arrangement that must have been as exciting for the trout and grayling as it was for the sheep. There are carvings of animals on the Norman doorway of the church, which has a font with a reptilian design reminiscent of that at Youlgreave. In the north aisle are more of the 'maidens' garlands' and gloves we previously came across at Ilam and Matlock. A 'black marble' tablet commemorates Henry Watson. In 1748 he organised what was probably the only business of its kind in England. Creating a quarry (now under the A6) at the foot of Kirk Dale, he hacked out a dark grey limestone with bituminous impurities and in a factory on the north bank of the Wye installed machinery – of his own invention – for cutting and polishing the stone and putting the shiny black product to ornamental use. The factory was closed in 1905 but there are samples of its work in the church here and in the chapel at Chatsworth. Inevitably the 'marble' was worked by Henry's nephew White Watson, a sculptor. Two other varieties of limestone mined between Ashford and Sheldon and used for decorative inlays were Rosewood Marble and Bird's Eye Marble.

As we realised at Sheldon, this area has more than its share of legend and mystery. On a secret curve in the Wye near Ashford is a somewhat incongruous limestone island in midstream. This is known as the Warren Stone. The story behind it concerns a shepherdess called Hedessa who was abducted and raped by Hulac Warren, the chief of a tribe of giants: whereupon the gods who look after the honour of young ladies chucked him in the river and turned him into stone. The narrow road from Ashford to Monsal Head has been in use for almost 2,000 years and was part of the Portway of Roman times. On its western flank, in a spinney behind a breach in the roadside wall, is a neglected, overgrown, tumbledown little graveyard. There was once a chapel in an adjoining field and a pool in a dip is said to have been used for baptising children. The chapel was pulled down at some time between 1844 and 1870 and the best stones became part of a new barn at Long Roods Farm up the road (where the farmer is considerably more affable than the geese on sentry duty). There has been no burial in that abandoned graveyard since 1916. The mystery is this: none of the headstones has any religious connotations, no denomination accepts responsibility for keeping the place tidy, and no one knows the full truth about the 'Infidels' Cemetery'.

For most people Little Longstone is a pleasing hamlet glimpsed through a window on the way to the suddenly spectacular view from a beauty spot that inspires a deep and lasting affection. Monsal Head stands steeply over a green, expansive loop in the Wye valley as the river swings round Putwell Hill and the 1,072ft Fin Cop (which has vestiges of the ramparts of a large hill fort probably built in the first century BC). Monsal Head thus commands a panorama of two different yet connected segments of the valley's gentle grandeur. The scene is wonderfully English: wooded, rocky hills, verdant meadows by the Wye, and an abundance of bird life. Once down in the valley, look out for kingfishers, weirs and water wheels. Amid all this natural splendour the cynosure of attention, oddly enough, is man-made: the mighty viaduct opened in 1863 much to John Ruskin's disgust. He waxed lyrical about the Wye valley and was bitter about the scars inflicted on it by the railway in order that 'every fool in Buxton can be at Bakewell in half an hour and every fool in Bakewell at Buxton; which you think a lucrative process of exchange'. The stations at Monsal Dale and Miller's Dale are closed and the railway has died. But that viaduct became such a familiar component of a much-loved view and such a massive memorial to the railway era that in the 1960s there were widespread protests when its demolition was proposed. In 1970 the viaduct was granted a preservation order – in spite of rumours of rotatory movements in Ruskin's grave.

Monsal Dale, Miller's Dale (the glen as distinct from the hamlet), and Chee Dale are the most delightful stretches of the Wye. The subsidiary Cressbrook Dale is interesting for its natural woodland and flora (including bird's-foot sedge) and an abundance of mosses with their associated tufa deposits. This is a good spot for the botanist – as is the old mining area above the southern slopes of Miller's Dale. Above Cressbrook Dale a child's skeleton was found in a tumulus on Hay Top, and Ravenscliffe Cave produced bear, reindeer and rhinoceros bones presumably discarded by Stone Age hunters.

At the foot of Cressbrook Dale is a striking sight in an attractive setting: a mill built in 1815. An unusual feature is the cupola, which contained a bell that was used to summon the workers. The first manager here was the self-educated poet William Newton (1750–1830). Born at Abney, five miles to the north, he was a carpenter like his father but also acquired mechanical skills and compensated for a limited education by reading widely – especially poetry. His own verses attracted the attention of another aspiring poet, Peter Cunningham, who was curate to Thomas Seward at Eyam. Seward's daughter Anna was an influential literary figure and she dubbed Newton 'The Derbyshire Minstrel', advanced his reputation as a poet, and also helped him raise enough money to become a partner in the mill. Newton was unusually humane in his treatment of boy apprentices, who were housed in a row of cottages facing Cressbrook Mill. In those days the factory system was harsh and the nearby Litton Mill (1782) was infamous for exploiting and mistreating cheap labour. Many of its apprentices died young and were buried in the churchyard at Tideswell, as was Newton.

Between the two old cotton mills is Water-cum-Jolly, a stretch of the Wye that for a mile or so winds beautifully through a gorge decorated with cliffs, woods, flowers, and (in season) such earnest fauna as climbers and botanists – often compatible breeds, as C. E. Montague so joyously demonstrated in my favourite short story, 'In Hanging Garden Gully'. The youth hostel at Ravenstor has a lovely location at the confluence of Miller's Dale and Tideswell Dale, amid dramatic residual evidence of the heaving contortions of that ancient sea bed and – note the dark streaks on the crags – volcanic action. Thanks to the National Trust Tideswell Dale is much tidier than it used to be and has been provided with picnic sites and a nature trail. The next branch valley, climbing out of the hamlet of Miller's Dale, is a rocky ravine that took its name from hillside vestiges of a monks' chapel. The remarkable thing about Monk's Dale is that it accommodates the smaller of two sections of the Peak District's most important nature reserve (the rest is in Lathkill Dale). Here are thirty-five private acres of rock, screes, scrub and grassland with a wide range of vegetation including very old natural woodland and the spring cinquefoil, Nottingham catchfly, and herb Paris.

There are lush weeds under the surface of the Wye and the flanking tree-clad slopes are rich in anemones, celandines and lilies. After a calm stretch by a meadow the river tumbles and twists round the spectacular, semi-circular bastion of Chee Tor: a riven 200ft crag, its steep whiteness spattered with tenacious foliage. On top of Chee Tor are faint reminders – best detected when the sun is low and the shadows sharp – of the fields and circular huts of a prehistoric settlement. At its foot is a variety of plant life, with an extensive stretch of Alpine currant. The chattering of jackdaws often dulls the chattering of the Wye. The gorge becomes deep and damp, with water dripping from mossy walls that seem to lean on you. Nature can be awfully beautiful and beautifully awful. Near the towering bulk of Topley Pike the Wye rejoins the A6.

Between Miller's Dale and Taddington is the hamlet of Priestcliffe, where an eighteenth-century farmer called George Smith had quite a tale to tell. He went to the fair at Buxton, drank too much, and later topped himself up at what used to be The Star in Taddington before tottering home in the moonlight. His story was that he got lost and was suddenly lifted high above the moon and thought he was drowning (logically explained by the fact that he fell into a pond after seeing the moon reflected in its surface). Then he saw a cave with a light in it. Curious, he went in and at the end of a winding passage found a metal-bound oak chest surmounted by bronze eagles and an inscription promising the contents – thousands of gold pieces – to any man brave enough to resist the eagles and raise the lid. Well, what would you have done? George Smith tried to raise the lid. But he was almost deafened by metallic screechings (bronze eagles or creaking hinges) and claimed that the eagles attacked him with beaks, talons and wings. He fled in terror and arrived home exhausted, frightened and sober.

A drunk's fevered imagination? Maybe. But it was possible that Roman booty with the usual aquiline insignia had been captured by the British and hidden in just such a cave. Alternatively there was the legend of Talcen's treasure. He was a Celtic prince who unsuccessfully wooed Alfred the Great's daughter Ethelfleda, the local Saxon ruler. She even turned down the treasure he offered. Piqued, Talcen joined the Danish opposition (their insignia was the raven) and when Saxons and Danes fought at Priestcliffe, Ethelfleda was killed. Overcome by remorse, Talcen went to live with a holy hermit in a cave by a spring – in the Priestcliffe vicinity.

The villagers put it all together: the basically impressive detail of George Smith's wild story, the conjecture about Romans, the legend of Talcen's treasure and the Danes, and the emblematic eagles and ravens. And for two days they made a systematic search under Smith's leadership. They drew blanks all the way, but the treasure may still be there. Just look out for the eagles . . .

More than 1,000ft up, at Horse Stead near Priestcliffe, is an example of terraced cultivation that may go back almost 1,400 years. Half a mile north of Chee Tor is Wormhill, a grassy, leafy village traditionally associated with trappers who hunted wolves in the days of the royal forest; William Bagshawe, 'the Apostle of the Peak', who preached his first sermon here; and England's first canal engineer, James Brindley (1716–72), who has a memorial stone over a well on the sunken green. There are stocks near by. Brindley was born in poverty in a humble cottage between the farming hamlet of Tunstead and Great Rocks Dale (since savaged by a mile and a quarter of man-made cliff, the largest limestone quarry in Europe). This was rough country inhabited by rough people – and one of them was Brindley's father, a peasant layabout who kept bad company and was more interested in bull-baiting than in doing a decent day's work. He neglected his family but luckily the children had a prudent mother with a sense of responsibility.

As a boy Brindley sometimes worked at Old Hall Farm, Wormhill, leading wagons loaded with sacks of grain to a grist mill down in Chee Dale. The mill's machinery so interested him that he committed the basics to memory and made a model of it by whittling pieces of wood. Until the age of 17 he was just a labourer with a mechanical flair. In 1733 he was apprenticed for seven years to a millwright (these were a versatile breed, the engineers of their day) at Gurnett, south of Macclesfield. At first he was such a bungler that at one time his indentures were almost cancelled. No one taught him – he had to work things out for himself. But he had a talent for repairing machinery and his skills became so obvious that he was put in charge of the workshop. When the master died, Brindley wound up the business and in 1742 began one of his own at Leek, mending machines and devising improvements. He was to make his name, though, as a civil – rather than mechanical – engineer. In 1759 he was consulted about the construction of the Duke of Bridgewater's canal for transporting coal from Worsley to Manchester. His imaginative plans included boat haulage through a tunnel from the mine, and an aqueduct over the River Irwell. When completed in 1761 this canal was the basis for England's entire system of inland navigation – and Brindley was to be largely responsible for more than 350 miles of it. He also suggested improvements in such revolutionary concepts as the steam engine and the use of water power.

The extraordinary thing is that throughout his life Brindley remained more or less illiterate, with no more than a rudimentary capacity to read or write. He could not benefit from drawings or written calculations. But he had a retentive and ingenious mind and a knack of swiftly identifying the nub of any engineering problem – and devising a solution. When confronted by a particularly baffling difficulty he often sought undisturbed quietness by retiring to bed for anything up to three days. When Brindley eventually got out of bed, it was all systems go. He was admired and respected, too, because of his integrity and his kind, unassuming, unaffected manner. Brindley's childhood home at Tunstead became a ruin in his own lifetime. But as if representing the spirit of Brindley's story, a young ash tree forced its way through the stone floor and grew to a formidable stature. They called it 'Brindley's Tree' and when it was destroyed in a storm they planted another, with a plaque close by.

North of Monsal Dale is the strictly linear village of Wardlow and, on the A623, Wardlow Mires, where a gibbet once cast its shadow. There was a brutal murder on New Year's Day, 1815, and a 21-year-old Tideswell man, Anthony

Lingard, was convicted and executed. As a warning to others his body was hung in chains on Peter's Stone, a detached block of limestone at the head of the dale that runs down to Cressbrook Mill. Litton, William Bagshawe's birthplace, is one of those villages in which hosiery manufacture was a thriving cottage industry in the eighteenth century. Like Tideswell (its larger neighbour), Litton has a well-dressing festival that incorporates a wakes carnival. Tideswell is also known for its old Shrove Tuesday custom of 'barring out' the school's headmaster pending the formal grant of a half-holiday.

There is some doubt whether Tideswell took its name from a 'tide' well (ebbing and flowing) or from a Saxon called Tidi. It stands at 1,000ft in a grey, humdrum setting and has an appropriately sturdy, no-nonsense look about it. The size of the place is impressive and the size of the church even more so. This 'cathedral' of the Peak is far too grand for its modern role. But we have to remember that Tideswell was the centre of a network of ancient tracks in a thinly populated area; that it was granted a charter for a market and fair as long ago as 1251 and simultaneously became a bustling market town and the hub of an independent parish; and that it was the seat of courts for trying those accused of breaking the strict laws of the royal forest of the Peak. Edward I, the last king to take an active interest in preserving the forest, spent three days here during a hunting trip in 1275. The wool trade and lead mining brought prosperity to this already important medieval town and the huge new church built between 1320 and 1380 was by no means as incongruous then as it seems now. The church is impressive inside and out. Many of its furnishings and carvings were the work of local craftsmen, the Hunstone family, who still have a workshop overlooking the market square and still specialise in ecclesiastical wood-carving. The medieval relics include a sedilia and piscina, a font (at one time dumped in the churchyard and used for mixing paint), and the tomb of Sir Sampson

Meverill, who owned the manor of Tideswell and had an adventurous military career in France in the days when Joan of Arc was causing so much fuss. As we know, the churchyard contains the graves of those poor apprentices from Litton Mill and, near a sundial, that of William Newton (whose eldest son financed the provision of a healthier water supply for the town).

Two inns to note are the George, with its striking eighteenth-century windows, and (at the crossroads half a mile north-east) the Anchor, which has an enviable range of malt whiskies and sherries and prudently serves the formidably potent Old Tom Ale in 'pony' glasses (a third of a pint). This is certainly a suitable location for supporting traditional brewing methods. Wheston has some of those longhouse-type farm buildings that put people and livestock under one roof and on the western side of this hamlet is the shaft of a fifteenth-century cross. At the Tideswell end of Wheston the base of another cross is now known as the Wishing Stone.

In the angle formed by the A6 as it weaves in and out of Buxton are Fairfield, which at more than 1,000ft has one of the highest golf courses in England, and Water Swallows, which took its name from a vanishing stream that reappeared three miles away in Chee Dale. To the north is Dove Holes. We have already noted its limestone quarries and old tramway. This drab village on a busy trunk road is also distinguished on the map by the words 'Bull Ring', which refer to a New Stone Age henge behind the church. It must have been similar to Arbor Low in size, shape and function; but centuries ago the stones were broken up and used for building and the site is now tricky to identify. Dove Holes yielded further prehistoric relics in the bones of a mastodon, a sabre-toothed tiger, and a rhinoceros. You will need a lively imagination to equate all this with the village as it is today.

Between Dove Holes and Buxton the Roman road known as Batham Gate veers north-east past the isolated village of

Peak Forest (even its railway station was more than two miles away). The royal forest covered about 180 square miles and had three wards: Longdendale in the north, Hopedale in the south-east, and Campagna in the south-west. Its northern and eastern boundaries were the Etherow and Derwent – as far south as the Bamford area. Then south-west to Tideswell and the Wye, across to the Goyt, and back north to the Etherow. It was wild, open country, but thickly wooded in places. The people were kicked out and the forest was reserved for royal hunting parties pursuing wolves, boars and a fierce breed of deer. There were cruel penalties for breaking the forest laws and one of the smaller courts, known as swainmotes, is believed to have sat just outside the village of Peak Forest at Chamber Farm. From the fourteenth century onwards the forest's functions became less important, its laws less severe. Poaching and deer rustling increased (most of it done by the upper classes, even the nobility and clergy) and the land gradually fell into private ownership. By the end of the fifteenth century there was little left to preserve, through Henry VII and Henry VIII did their best, and by the end of the seventeenth century the forest was no longer even a formality – just a scattering of memories, names and traditions.

The other interesting thing about the village of Peak Forest is the church: founded in 1657, rebuilt in 1877–78, and unusually dedicated to King Charles the Martyr. From 1665 onwards the minister had the power to grant marriage licences and many runaway couples found Peak Forest more convenient than Gretna Green. This practice declined after the Marriage Act of 1753 but survived until 1804. Then, like the royal hunting reserve, it became a piece of Peak Forest history. Another chapter had ended.

5
The Village that Almost Died

FROM ELDON HILL TO BRADWELL, EYAM AND BIG MOOR
See map pages 126–127

Sparrowpit, the junction of an assortment of roads at 1,217ft, is nominally unusual for its own name and that of the Wanted Inn, formerly the Devonshire Arms, which was called the Unwanted Inn when it was put up for sale and no one would buy it, and the Wanted Inn when someone finally did. The 1,543ft Eldon Hill ('Elve's Hill') represents another conflict of character. Its western slopes have been wounded and disfigured by quarrying but ancient man buried his dead on the summit and high on the southern flank is the accidental grave of many wandering beasts, an astonishing hole in the ground renowned as the Peak District's most alarming natural curiosity.

Eldon Hole is the largest open pothole in the Peak District and used to be known as the Bottomless Pit. About 120ft long and 20ft wide, it plunges 180ft and modern cavemen can then explore a cavern system that goes even deeper. The first man known to touch bottom, in 1770, found it already covered by loose rocks tossed down by visitors (complete walls had disappeared) and stinking with rotten sheep. In 1958 a landowner who lost a heifer down there was so cross that he dallied with the idea of blowing in the hole and sealing it. And beasts have not been the only victims. About 300 years ago a villain confessed on the scaffold that while guiding a traveller he had robbed the chap and then chucked him into Eldon Hole. The first voluntary descendant – one uses 'voluntary' in a relative sense – was reputedly a reluctant but hard-up sixteenth-century peasant hired for the purpose by the Earl of Leicester. He was lowered on a rope and, when hauled back after a suitable interval for contemplation, had been transformed into a white-haired, gibbering idiot who was to die a few days later. A more engaging tradition concerns a goose who flew down Eldon Hole and was given up for lost but later emerged from the Peak Cavern (always associated with the Devil) more than two miles away. The bird's feathers had been singed by the fires of hell . . .

The hamlet of Brough, on the A625, stands on the River Noe – known to the Romans as the Anava – at the junction of the roads they built between Sheffield and Melandra (near Glossop) and between Buxton and Brough. The name Brough means a fortified place and here the Romans built an auxiliary fort manned by about 500 French troops, the First Cohort of Aquitanians. They called it Anavio. General Agricola, who governed Britain from AD 78 to 85, extended Roman rule into Scotland but had a lot of bother on the way – not least with the fierce and restless tribe of Brigantes who roamed the southern Pennines. Anavio was built in 78–79, strengthened about 158, and was useful in the suppression of two uprisings. But its always modest role ended in the fourth century because pressure from the northern Saxons was becoming too much of a nuisance. It has now vanished from the landscape because the excavations were later filled in. But Brough still has its corn mill, more than 600 years old. And homesick visitors from the West Country can find solace at the Traveller's Rest, which serves sixteen brands of cider and only one brand of beer.

East of the Brough–Bradwell road is a grassy, earthen rampart called Grey Ditch, which was constructed at some time in the first twelve centuries but has yet to be dated more accurately. It falls from Bradwell Edge to Batham Gate, the Roman road from Buxton, and might conceivably have been an attempt to check the Roman advance. The name Bradwell may be an adaptation of 'broad wall'. It has been alleged, especially by Castletonians, that their neighbours the 'Bradderites' are descended from French and Italian convicts – including political offenders – who were deported by the Romans and forced to work in lead mines on Bradwell Moor and live in stone huts near the mines. Bradwell certainly developed as a colony of miners (many kept cows, too), who needed timber for mining and smelting and were sometimes in trouble with the law for pinching it from Edale and the now woodless Pin Dale. In 1806 the miners discovered Bagshaw Cavern, with its fossils, stalactites and stalagmites; but this was not to become a 'show' cave like those at Castleton. Bradwell also became a quarrying village and packhorse trains used to come down the hill laden with limestone for the kilns in Smalldale. It also had a hat-making business and the felt 'Bradder beavers' were used by generations of miners and became widely popular. The village even acquired a small piece of the optical industry, making telescopes, binoculars and spectacles. Samuel Fox (1815–87), the inventor of the umbrella frame, was a Bradwell man. The son of a weaver's shuttle-maker, he went into the trade of wire-drawing, making hackle pins for combing wool. Then he devised a hollow-drawn steel wire for umbrella frames. In 1840 he went to Stocksbridge, near Sheffield, and it was there that he made his name and his fortune. But his roots were in Bradwell.

This area has long had more than its share of smoking industry: lead smelting, lime kilns, and nowadays its controversial cement works. The business based in one of the world's largest limestone quarries is the biggest industrial unit in the national park and dates from 1929, when the park was still a dream. The great scar in the hillside has been camouflaged by trees but there was nothing they could do to hide a 400ft chimney, which puffs away as incongruously as a pipe-smoker at a church service. The religious analogy is apt because the Hope Valley is something of a Mecca for devotees of natural beauty – and that chimney spoils the prospect for miles.

Bradwell's non-conformist chapel, built in 1662, had its interior wrecked by a Roman Catholic mob – inspired by the Jacobite rising – one night in 1715 while the miners were sleeping. Later it was damaged by fire. Bradwell had no church until 1868. Hazlebadge Hall, now incorporated in a roadside farmstead at the top of Bradwell Dale, dates from 1549 but has been disguised by resurfacing and a new roof. It is one more reminder of Bradwell's diversified and eventful history, which the village celebrates every August with a well-dressing festival that includes a carnival and barbecue.

Between Hazlebadge Hall and Little Hucklow is Intake Farm, which owes its name to the practice – going back to medieval times – of taming previously uncultivated land and 'taking it in' to a farm holding. On either side of Great Hucklow are Grindlow, an ancient settlement that has a prehistoric barrow, and the 1,300ft Burrs Mount – formerly an oval hill fort with a double ditch, but now serving a sharply contrasting purpose as part of a landing area for the visually unexpected gliders that sweep gently across this high, mostly bare country. In addition to its gliders Great Hucklow was formerly renowned for the dramatic company formed in 1927 by the playwright L. du Garde Peach, who directed this enterprising venture until 1971, when he seemed to feel that its life should end with his own. In any case male actors had become scarce. To the south-east the carolling village of Foolow has been suspended in time. Gathered round a green and a pond, it still has wells, a fifteenth-century cross, and a bull ring (a Bull's Head, too). Nothing much happens at Foolow. Perhaps nothing much ever did. The nearby Silly Dale may have taken its name from the old meaning of the word silly: a blessed innocence.

North-east of the Hucklows is the thriving little community of Abney, where William Newton the 'minstrel' was born at Cockey Farm. Abney lies remotely in a hollow amid high, moorland country, alongside a clough that has an uncommon variety of ferns. This is such an ancient area of settlement that Offerton Hall and Highlow Hall, both sixteenth century in origin, are comparatively modern. South of Abney Low is Bretton Clough, which has had a strange hold over me since the days when, as Boy Scouts, we used to make it the turning point of an annual New Year's Day ramble. It is an odd, secret little place, appealing because of its character rather than its beauty. There is evidence of landslips, a confused array of shaly little hills, a few deserted farm buildings, a variety of plants, a general air of miniaturised neglect. In 1745 cattle were hidden here from Bonnie Prince Charlie's foraging Highlanders, deserters included, who stole whatever they wanted. But my favourite Bretton Clough story concerns a farmer who went to Highlow Mill with his donkey for a bag of corn. On the return trip the donkey refused to carry the load any farther than Stoke Ford, kicking it off every time the farmer tried to put it on. So the chap had no choice but to put the load on his own back and let the donkey follow him home. That was vexing enough. But the farmer discovered that the load was getting lighter – because the donkey had bitten a hole in the sack and was eating the spilling corn. Purple with rage, the man rushed into his house and demanded: 'Where's my gun? I'm going to shoot that donkey this minute.' But his wife had seen them coming, had read the hotly coloured signs of anger – and had hidden the gun. Just one frustration after another. We all have days like that.

Many of the Bretton miners had smallholdings and kept cobs, and they held Sunday morning race meetings. The Barrel Inn, which stands at 1,300ft and retains much of the mood of its 1637 origins, was once run by the Bennetts. One of the family, a miner, had a bet at the mine that he could wheel a ton of lead ore in a barrow. He did so, won his bet – and then went home to the Barrel and died. The miners ran a burial club at the Barrel. The Romans used to do the same thing, just to make sure there would be enough in the kitty to give them a decent send-off to the next world. But the Barrel burial club had an unusual rule: a member had to give two weeks' notice of death or the money would not be paid. As no one ever made a claim, the miners disposed of the fund by having a party at the Barrel every Christmas.

On the edge of Eyam Moor, overlooking Highlow Brook, is the Bronze Age circle of Wet Withins, more than 30 yards in diameter, with blocks of gritstone surrounded by an earthen bank. There are other, smaller circles in the same area, plus a few barrows. To the south the straight and steep Sir William Hill links Bretton with Grindleford and at one point rises beyond 1,400ft. This was constructed in 1757 as part of the turnpike between Sheffield, Buxton and Manchester. It was named after Bess of Hardwick's grandson, Sir William Cavendish, who fought for Charles I at the Civil War battle of Marston Moor in 1644. He lived a mile downstream from Grindleford at Stoke Hall, which has since been rebuilt and turned into a hotel.

Halfway up Sir William Hill a road branches south towards Eyam and passes the surviving structures of two lead mines. To the west was Ladywash Mine, recently worked for fluorspar and barytes, and to the east – at the top of the wooded slopes of Mag Clough – was the New Engines Mine. Last worked in 1884, this had a 1,092ft shaft, the deepest in the Peak District. In the middle of Eyam the Glebe Mines were exploited for fluorspar until 1979. But before getting down into Eyam we should note that, in a grassy cul-de-sac on the right about half a mile south of Sir William Hill, there is a stone water trough called Mompesson's Well. During the 1665–66 plague Eyam put itself into quarantine and arranged for provisions to be brought to special points on the village outskirts, where coins (in payment) were left in water disinfected by the addition of vinegar. Mompesson's Well was the best-known location for these transactions.

Eyam, pronounced 'Eem', has not changed much since the terrible tragedy of the plague. The much-told story is still awfully moving, especially when considered in its actual context. The Black Death, bubonic plague transmitted to man by fleas from black rats, swept across Europe from the fourteenth century onwards. In 1665 it killed a tenth of London's inhabitants and wiped out entire villages. At Eyam the dead numbered 259 out of 76 families, a total population of about 350: which meant that only one villager in four survived.

West of the church are some seventeenth-century gritstone cottages. The 'Plague Cottage' was then occupied by a miner's widow, a Mrs Cooper, her two sons, and a lodger – a travelling tailor called George Vicars. In September 1665, a box of clothing material from London was delivered here and Vicars opened it. Within four days he was dead. Mrs Cooper's sons died, too. After that the people of Eyam perished fast except when the plague abated during the winter. The village had two ministers. One was the young rector, William Mompesson, a scholarly man who had been in Eyam for only six months and found his life-style there somewhat deficient in the comfort and gentility to which he had been accustomed. The other was Thomas Stanley, a nonconformist who had been ejected from the living after the Restoration, in 1660, but had remained in Eyam. Mompesson evacuated his two children but his wife insisted on staying with him during Eyam's self-imposed isolation: an initiative taken by Mompesson to prevent the plague from spreading elsewhere. Eyam's brave but possibly misguided sacrifice meant that it paid a far higher price than most other villages afflicted by the plague.

The churchyard was soon bursting with nameless graves and could take no more. So graves were dug in fields and gardens and families buried their own dead. The Riley graves (Riley was the name of the location rather than the people living there) are well-known examples. John Hancock and his three sons and three daughters all died in a week, in August 1666, and were buried there by his wife, who then joined her surviving son in Sheffield. In the orchard of Riley House Farm is the family grave of seven Talbots. That sort of thing was happening all over Eyam. At least one woman had gone crazy. Across the road from 'Plague Cottage' lived the Siddal family. The father and five of the six children died in October 1665, leaving the mother and one daughter. In April the daughter died – and the mother, demented, by grief, went to live outdoors in Cucklet (or 'Cussy') Delf, a green little valley that runs down from Eyam to Middleton Dale. By this time the church had been closed and Mompesson was preaching to his dwindling congregation from an arched recess in the rocky wall of the Delf. Thus 'Cucklet Church' and 'Pulpit Rock' found their way into Eyam's vocabulary.

The last plague victim died in October 1666, thirteen months after that box of material had been delivered to George Vicars. The dead included Mompesson's wife Catherine, whose tomb is sheltered by a yew in a churchyard. Both ministers survived. Mompesson left soon afterwards to take the living of Eakring, in Nottinghamshire, but Stanley stayed in Eyam until he died in 1670.

The plague years had an ironic, bitterly macabre epilogue. Children still join hands to sing a happy little nursery rhyme:

> Ring a ring o'roses,
> A pocket full of posies,
> A-tishoo! A-tishoo!
> We all fall down.

The ring of roses was a rash on the chest, the first symptom of the plague. Posies of fragrant herbs were carried in an attempt to keep the affliction at bay. Sneezing was the last symptom before the fatal swelling developed.

Most children have no idea what the words represent. But the children of Eyam know – because the families of the dead are all around them, and at the end of August a memorial service is held in Cucklet Delf after a procession from the church. On the preceding Saturday there is a well-dressing festival (this and the contemporaneous ceremony at Wormhill's Brindley Well are the last of the year). The week's celebrations also include a carnival and sheep-roast.

Eyam was a Saxon settlement founded in the eighth century or early in the ninth. The cross in the churchyard dates from this period, combines Christian and pagan symbols, and is the best-preserved relic of its kind in the Peak District. Found in the hills above Eyam, it was brought down to the churchyard but lay there neglected for many years until 1778 when the philanthropist and prison reformer, John Howard, visited Eyam and was so impressed by the cross that he took the initiative in restoring it to proper dignity. Sections of the church go back to the thirteenth century and other notable old buildings include the Miners Arms (1630) and Eyam Hall (1676). There are stocks on the little green opposite the Hall. Down the hill, overlooking a traffic island, is a house with a primrose-painted door. This used to be the Foresters Arms and set into the surface of the lane outside is a metal plate that can be partly raised to reveal a bull ring. The 'sport' of bull-baiting consisted of chaining the animal to such a ring and setting the dogs on it until they worried the bull to death. Eyam has a museum where much of its history can be studied in detail. The village used to produce shoes and minor poets. One of its rectors, Thomas Seward, fancied himself as a playwright, poet, and author. Peter Cunningham, his curate for eighteen years, was another enthusiastic versifier – and the first to appreciate William Newton's talent. Seward's daughter Anna, born at the rectory in 1747, was to become known as 'The Swan of Lichfield' (where she spent most of her sixty-one years and in the process developed a somewhat antipathetic relationship with Samuel Johnson). Her verse was mediocre, sentimental, and affected but was also fashionable: partly, no doubt, because a poetess was inherently extraordinary. Miss Seward was tall and personable, with a warm, vivacious personality. But she refused all offers of marriage and devoted herself to the literary life, social duties, and a prolific correspondence.

Much of this was directed to Sir Walter Scott, whom she greatly admired. He visited her at Lichfield two years before her death, but found her letters effusive and was embarrassed when she made him her literary executor. Eyam's versifying era was extended by Richard Furness, born there in 1791, who became a poet, preacher, soldier, and schoolmaster (at Dore, south-west of Sheffield).

Grindleford, where Burbage Brook joins the Derwent, has a superb setting and has been familiar to generations of ramblers. These pour off the trains that emerge from Totley Tunnel, which was completed in 1893 after its construction had been hampered by flooding. At three miles and 950 yards this is England's longest tunnel except for the Severn. The Dore and Chinley line, opened in 1894, greatly improved access to the Hope Valley and Edale for the Peak District's flanking urban masses. They blinked into the daylight from the Cowburn Tunnel in the west or Totley Tunnel in the east. So Edale and Grindleford acquired special places in the affections of all the lads and lasses escaping to beauty from the workaday greyness of Manchester and Sheffield. They met in the middle and teased each other about being born on the 'wrong' side of the Pennines. They still do.

Padley Mill, handy for Grindleford station and Burbage Brook, may have been the first wire-drawing mill in England. Along a rough track from the station are Padley Chapel and vestigial walls that give us an idea of the ground-floor plan of Padley Hall. Robert Eyre came home from Agincourt in 1415, married Joan Padley, and built a manor house here. Part of it was later converted into a chapel. They were Roman Catholics and had fourteen children. The male line expired but one of their descendants, Anne Eyre, married Sir Thomas Fitzherbert of Norbury, near Ashbourne. They settled at Padley but as distinguished and steadfast Catholics – at a time when Mary Queen of Scots was in custody in the same area – they were regarded with disapproval and suspicion. Sir Thomas was arrested in 1571 and died in the Tower of

London after twenty years in prison. Meantime his brother John was looking after the manor. It was suspected that Mass was being celebrated at Padley (there may have been some traitorous skulduggery by John's eldest son, a Protestant, who wanted to get his hands on the estate) and the manor was raided on the orders of the Earl of Shrewsbury, the Lord Lieutenant of Derbyshire. That raid took place at night, while the household were sleeping, on 12 July 1588: exactly a week before the Spanish Armada was sighted off the Lizard.

It was not a healthy time to be a Catholic in England. Priests ordained abroad were legally outlaws guilty of high treason and subject to the death penalty – as were those who sheltered or assisted them. Two such priests, both ordained at Reims, were found hiding at Padley in buttresses disguised as part of the chimney structure. One was Robert Ludlam, born near Sheffield, and the other Nicholas Garlick, who had been a Tideswell schoolmaster for seven years. The priests, John Fitzherbert, four of his children, and ten retainers were arrested and taken to Derby. On 24 July Garlick and Ludlam were hanged, drawn and quartered at St Mary's Bridge and the segments were then displayed in public (that night they were recovered by Catholic sympathisers and subsequently given a decent burial). John Fitzherbert was also condemned to death but died in prison.

Padley Hall was demolished in 1650, much of the stone being used to build a farmhouse near by. The chapel, neglected, was used as a barn and a cowshed until 1932, when it was bought, restored, and reconsecrated by Roman Catholics. In July 1933, Mass was celebrated there for the first time since 1588. It is still used for the same purpose and if you happen to be in the vicinity around 12 July you may find what seems to be an unusually genteel football crowd, including many priests, flooding along that track between station and chapel. Because every year there is a pilgrimage to honour the martyrs Garlick and Ludlam.

Whatever your religion, this is good walking country.

You can make for Hathersage along the Derwent valley or savour the more secluded pleasures of Burbage Brook and Padley Wood – a ramble remarkable for a variety of birds and mosses, tenacious fragments of medieval woodland, and eventually the expansive and diverse delights of the National Trust's Longshaw estate. In addition to its own natural beauty, Longshaw commands the prospect of a great deal more. It accommodates sheepdog trials in September and, when the winter is hard enough, some hazardously amateurish and totally unofficial ice-skating on its attractive little lake. As my brother and I vividly recall from our energetic youth, the estate is largely maintained by voluntary working parties who set about such chores as tree-felling, logging up, burning, ditching, and trying to prevent innocent or mischievous visitors from doing anything daft. Longshaw is no bad place for a spot of courting, either, if you are still playing in that league.

Longshaw Lodge, which was begun about 1830 and later extended, was originally the Duke of Rutland's shooting lodge. During the grouse-shooting season his house parties were sometimes so well attended that the overflow of guests had to sleep on the floor at the Fox House Inn. When I recently passed that way the inn had a striking but misleading sign depicting a fox in the foreground. A farmer or shepherd would be more accurately appropriate because the place was named after a Fox, not a fox. The original structure was a shepherd's cottage built about 1773 by George Fox, who farmed at Callow Farm on the other side of Hathersage and had sheep-grazing rights in the upper Burbage valley.

Mind you, this is a traditional breeding area for foxes and was hunting country until the 1920s. Foxes (and rock-climbers, too) simply had to thrive in the presence of a dozen moorland escarpments or 'edges' stretching for almost twenty miles in a jagged, wandering line from the Derwent Reservoir in the north to Chatsworth in the south. It must be an exhilarating experience to tread all those heights in the course of a single day's walk, with a well-earned pint or two at the end of it. To motorists, perhaps the most familiar are Froggatt Edge, Curbar Edge, and Baslow Edge (really a continuous rocky ridge), which make up the stark skyline towering over the Derwent and the little communities of Froggatt and Curbar. There is a Bronze Age stone circle on Froggatt Edge. At the upper end of Curbar, where the village merges with the moor, five simple slabs lie in a hollow among heather and bracken. They mark the graves of a family killed in 1632 by the plague that was to devastate Eyam thirty-three years later. It has been suggested that a quaintly designed structure at the bottom of a nearby private garden may have been used to isolate plague victims, but the place is more likely to have been built in the eighteenth century. It was certainly used as a lock-up, where prisoners could be detained until they were taken to proper jails, and also served as a modest, one-up one-down dwelling until shortly before the Second World War. The oddest thing is that a conical roof has been neatly constructed onto an otherwise square building, which demanded some intricate internal architecture. A stone in Curbar's churchyard marks the grave of a carpenter, preacher and renowned angler called George Butcher, who died in 1875. He was the Izaak Walton of the Derwent.

But get up on the tops and enjoy the view. At the southern end of Baslow Edge is the Eagle Stone, a 14ft chunk of gritstone that was isolated when the stuff around it was eroded. One theory about its name concerns the Saxon god Aigle, who reputedly amused himself by tossing about boulders that men could not move. Baslow had a tradition that local lads were not mature enough to marry until they had climbed the Eagle Stone. It stands near the junction of two bridle paths. One of these, which until 1816 served as a link between Baslow and Sheffield, passes Wellington's Monument, a conspicuous landmark that commands spectacular views. It was erected in 1866 on the initiative of a Baslow antiquarian who, as a young man, had served in the Duke of Wellington's Regiment. He thought the 1805 Nelson's Monument on Birchen Edge, across the valley, should have a mate to keep it company.

The monuments are separated by the Bar Brook valley, the A621, and Gardom's Edge (John Gardom of Bubnell, near Baslow, built the original Calver Mill). The climbers on Gardom's Edge provide perilously distracting entertainment for passing motorists. The crags were formerly quarried for millstones and there are still a few about. Up the moor just behind them is Birchen Edge, which was my own favourite climbing area. There is not much of it and the routes are relatively easy. But the rock is warm, friendly and adhesive, and the panorama superb. I used to go up there twice a week with a well-built chimney sweep who, in emergency, clambered over roofs to rescue his brush. Birchen Edge became a second home to us, a private gymnasium. When a sufficiency of modest ambitions had been fulfilled, we propped our backs against that honest rock, stretched our legs in the heather, and let the birds and breezes sing to us while we emptied flasks and sandwich boxes and rested our muscles. The days tasted like wine.

A mile east of Birchen Edge is the crude, thirteenth-century Whibbersley Cross formerly associated with Beauchief Abbey, on the outskirts of Sheffield. It stands on the edge of a vast expanse of marsh and cotton grass called Leash Fen, the flattest moor and largest fen in the Peak District. Ramsley Moor, to the north, has the remnants of two more old crosses, and its neighbour Big Moor has Lady's Cross (formerly the intersection of two packhorse routes) and residual evidence of two stone circles. Swine Sty was a settlement where shale was worked to provide our Bronze Age ancestors with buttons and other sartorial trimmings. There are two reservoirs on this bleak moorland wilderness, but very little to tickle the aesthetic palate unless you have a taste for the vegetation prevalent in such soggy, upland environments. Until, that is, you get as far as White Edge, a commendable viewpoint east of the main escarpment. The name came from the White family. Early in the nineteenth century they cleared the land in the vicinity of that congenial pub, the Grouse Inn.

Totley Moor has visual surprises in the shape of ventilating shafts from the railway tunnel beneath it. On scanty evidence it has been suggested that about 3,000 years ago there may have been a settlement on Brown Edge. There was certainly a cairn in the middle of a level area enclosed by an earthen bank. Excavations brought to light pottery, flint tools and indications of five cremations more than a thousand years BC. To the north-east, just across the national-park boundary, some of Sheffield's luckier citizens live in the pleasant old village of Dore. Its green, the scene of a well-dressing festival, has a memorial suggesting that King Egbert of Wessex led his army to Dore in 829 and there confronted King Eanred of Northumbria, whose submission was part of the empire-building process that made Egbert the first king of England – all of it, as distinct from the previously fragmented kingdoms. We should suppress the wild speculation that in this story lie the roots of the word 'battledore'. The word-association game can be mischievous.

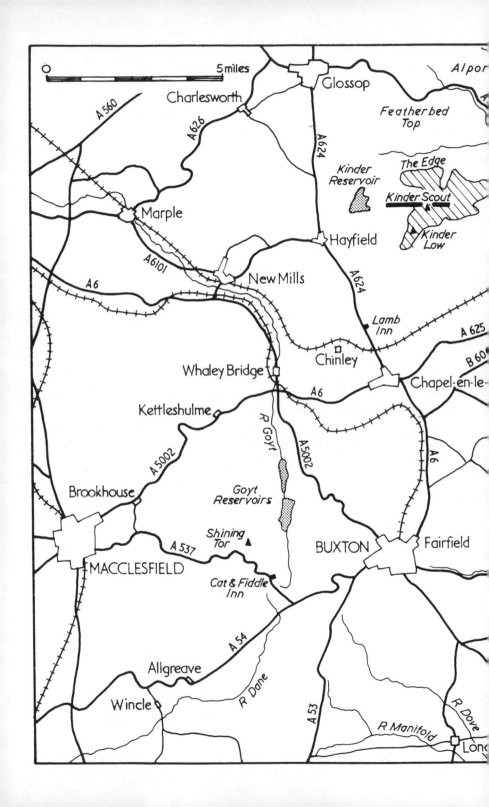

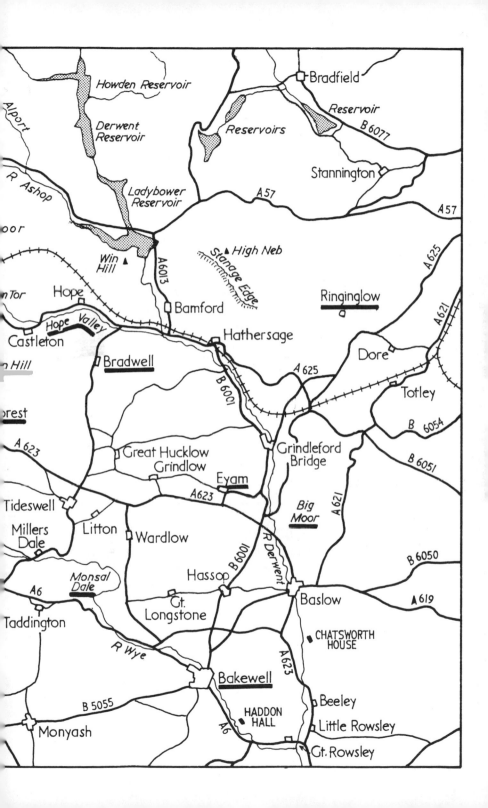

6
Little John and Jane Eyre

FROM RINGINGLOW TO THE HOPE VALLEY AND KINDER SCOUT
See map pages 170–171

We have just covered a stimulating stretch of no man's land between the limestone dales of the south and the wild, gritstone moorland of the north. The A625 and the Hope Valley mark a definite transition to the bleak grandeur of bog-trotters' country. Challenging, often hostile, it vies with the Lake District as the most popular rambling terrain in England: and can there be any wonder that city folk appreciate the contrast of high, empty, lonely places? The weather tends to be colder, wetter, and unpredictably nastier than that prevalent on the lower flanks of the Pennines. At the end of a rough day on the tops we gratefully tramp down to scattered villages that look tough, durable, capable of withstanding anything nature can throw at them. There is nothing fancy up here.

From Dore the national-park boundary runs north to Ringinglow and the Rivelin Valley. Ringinglow has a tiny mission church and, to the west, some old slate quarries. But what matters is the Round House and all it represents. Its tollbar was the hub of three important turnpikes that crossed the wilderness from Sheffield's Psalter Lane (once associated with the Cheshire salt trade and spelt without the 'p'). Two of these turnpikes date from 1757. The first, which fell into disuse when the Sheffield–Fox House road was opened in 1816, climbed south from Ringinglow across Houndkirk Moor and was known as Houndkirk Road. The coaches rattled on to Grindleford, then up Sir William Hill to Great Hucklow, Tideswell, Wormhill, and Buxton. The

(*above*) The Toad's Mouth, a huge boulder shaped like a squatting toad, stands by Burbage Brook and a sharp corner on the Sheffield–Hathersage road. Another curiosity, the hill-fort known as Carl Wark, is a short walk away; (*below*) Winnats Pass, a steep, windswept gorge near Castleton. This old packhorse and turnpike route is supposedly haunted by the ghosts of two runaway lovers murdered by miners in 1758

Two views from one of the Peak District's most impressively panoramic short walks, along Derwent Edge. The photograph below shows the Salt Cellar, one of many bizarre rock formations

other 1757 turnpike went west across Burbage Moor to Hathersage, Castleton, and up Winnats Pass to Sparrowpit, Chapel-en-le-Frith and Manchester. The third coach road, dating from 1777, branched off the Hathersage turnpike just below Overstones Farm and descended from the foot of Stanage Edge to Bamford and Ashopton, a village since drowned by the Ladybower Reservoir.

Nowadays a busier route out of Sheffield is the A57 via the attractive Rivelin Valley, where dams and woodland are hemmed in by swelling hills. On Rivelin Rocks the views are, in my experience, more admirable than the climbing. One day a chunk of rock broke off the main mass. Its fall was swiftly followed by mine because I was standing on it at the time (had it not been for that strong-armed chimney sweep, who held me dangling like a fish on a line, you might never have read this cautionary tale). There is a slight Scottish accent about the pretty scenery up Wyming Brook, a popular spot among Sheffield folk. It connects Rivelin with Redmires, where there are three reservoirs (the one in the middle, built in 1835–36, was the first of its size in the Peak District). Unlikely though it seems, Redmires had a racecourse from 1875 to 1877.

Running south-west from the reservoirs is the Long Causeway, which is believed to have been a Roman road connecting Anavio (Brough) to one of the settlements in the Sheffield area. The existing causeway was probably paved in the eighteenth century, on a Roman base, and was essentially a packhorse route for transporting millstones to Sheffield. Abandoned millstones can be seen in the vicinity of Stanage Edge and, farther south, Millstone Edge. This was a debilitating trade and millstone-makers used to say that the harder you worked the sooner you died. Scattered along the top of Stanage Edge are twenty-nine drinking holes, which were all numbered so that the keepers could be sure they did not miss any. Bog water is too acid for grouse, so these holes were cut in the gritstone, filled by the keepers, and additionally replenished from little channels that caught the rain. Stanage Edge is more than three miles long and in places rises to 1,500ft. Renowned among climbers for the variety and severity of its challenges, the cliff is a strikingly rugged sight and commands exhilarating views. The Long Causeway meets it halfway, which has been a busy spot for centuries because several ancient tracks converge here.

At the southern extremity of Stanage Edge the head waters of Burbage Brook are crossed by the modern version of the old Ringinglow turnpike. Burbage Bridge is an enchanting place and deservedly popular. There are times when the great sweeps of cotton grass on Hallam Moors look like summer snowfields. By contrast the brook chuckles and tumbles down a rocky glen into a broad, curving valley massively protected by Burbage Rocks on one side and Higger Tor and Carl Wark on the other. The path down that valley, eventually passing abandoned millstone quarries, is plainly called the Green Drive. The range of colour is so wide and so subtly blended, and its context so striking, that on a good day the beauty of Burbage can be breathtaking.

The name Higger Tor may be a corruption of 'higher' or a throwback to some prehistoric god: 'Hugaer' or 'Yggr'. It stands at 1,261ft, commands impressively extensive views, and is edged by strangely eroded rocks. One day, at the roadside behind Higger Tor, my brother and I saw the aerial of a portable television set protruding from a parked car occupied by a family with unmoving eyeballs. Television seems a poor substitute for the music of birds and streams and the visual impact of the upper Burbage but as the saying goes, 'There's nowt so queer as folk'. Lower down the valley is Carl Wark, one of the Peak District's outstanding hill-forts because nature made it that way. Here was a flat-topped knoll with ready-made defensive walling in the form of a conveniently shaped cliff. All our ancestors had to do was rearrange and reinforce the existing stonework and – on the upper, vulnerable side – build an earthen bank and a dry-stone wall made of the most suitable boulders that happened to be lying around. What is left of that wall must be one of the oldest of its kind in England. At its southern end was the entrance and guard chamber. There was only room for a small camp and Carl Wark has yielded no convincing testimony to its exact period. At first it was thought to be an Iron Age structure but modern opinion supports a later date: probably the fifth or sixth century, when England was 'up for grabs' because the Romans had just gone home.

Burbage Brook darts under a sharp corner on the A625 at the Toad's Mouth, a huge boulder that really does look like a squatting toad. A mile along the road to Hathersage is a second sharp corner with another hazardous visual distraction. This is called 'The Surprise' because, as the road dodges through a gap in Millstone Edge and swings right, it is as if unseen hands had suddenly hurled back the curtains to show us a new world. Totally different. Totally unexpected. Seconds ago we were driving along an intimate stretch of gently sloping moorland. Now we are poised over a vastly wider, deeper, longer view – mile after distant mile of valleys and receding hills, prettiness and grandeur. The startling transition from sterility to fertility happens in a few yards with no effort other than a gear change (down).

Little John and Charlotte Brontë's alter ego, Jane Eyre, knew the same Shangri La: because we are driving down to Hathersage.

Little John's grave lies in the shade of a yew in Hathersage churchyard. It is said that when he realised he was dying he propped himself up by the wall of his cottage, east of the churchyard, shot an arrow as best he could, and said he should be buried where it fell. The surprising and satisfying thing is that such a man almost certainly did exist. The evidence in favour of his story is convincing if largely circumstantial, whereas the evidence against it is speculative. The cottage, for example, was still there late in the nineteenth century and the old lady who occupied it in 1847 said that the former owners had told her that Little John died in it and was buried in the churchyard. It is further claimed that after his death his bow of spliced yew, some arrows, chain armour and a green cap were displayed in the church: and such equipment, obviously used by a renowned forester of exceptional stature, was indeed hanging in the church more than 300 years ago. The cap and bow were among the accoutrements of the man who played the role of Little John in the village's May Day festival. The bow was tested in 1715 and needed a draw of 160lb (the tester shot a deer with it). The Stanhope family, of Cannon Hall, between Barnsley and Denby Dale, became the local squires and took home everything except the cap, for safe keeping. The equipment was never seen again. In 1780 the grave was opened by Stanhope's cousin and a thigh bone was found that was measured at $28\frac{1}{2}$in. The cousin took the bone home, too, but had a series of misfortunes until it was returned. At that time the headstone and footstone were moved closer together: so the grave, large even now, was formerly even larger.

In the eighteenth century, too, the story was investigated as thoroughly as was possible and some plausible embellishments were added. It seems that there was a Hathersage nailmaker called John Little (the transposition of names would have been as obvious a joke then as it would be now) of extraordinary stature, strength and prowess. He fought in Simon de Montfort's defeated army at the Battle of Evesham in 1265 and was therefore outlawed – and joined Robin Hood in the woods. Both died of old age. It was after Robin's death that John Little or Little John returned to his cottage at Hathersage and, soon afterwards, measured his length in the grave we see today. All that is acceptable except where it touches on the romanticised legend of Robin Hood. No one has been able to get at the truth of that. What is interesting, though, is that the first detailed 'history' of Robin Hood related to south-west Yorkshire: a neck of the woods that would have been familiar to any outlawed nailmaker from Hathersage. Let us leave it there save for a relevantly permissible pun: the dead lie in graves, but graves seldom lie about the dead.

The facts about Charlotte Brontë (1816–55) are solid. She maintained a lifelong friendship with a schoolmate called Ellen Nussey who lived at Birstall (Batley). Miss Nussey had a brother, Henry, who became vicar of Hathersage and in the summer of 1845, while he and his wife were on their honeymoon, Miss Nussey went to Hathersage to sort out the vicarage for the newly-weds: assemble furniture, decorate rooms and appoint servants. In June her shy, short-sighted, delicate, brilliant little friend Miss Brontë came down from Haworth to help her and stayed for three weeks. *Jane Eyre* was published two years later and almost a quarter of it concerned Hathersage (Morton) and was a fanciful, semi-autobiographical reconstruction of Miss Brontë's own character and experience and a distorted reflection of people and places she knew. Let us consider a few examples.

Among the four or five proposals of marriage made to Miss Brontë, one was from a publishers' editor who had to go to Bombay to open a branch of the house and another, in 1839, was from Henry Nussey, then a stiff, solemn, humourless curate. He later became a missionary. The parallel with the St John Eyre Rivers of the novel, a bigoted if well-meaning prig who was setting off for a missionary life in the East and wanted Jane Eyre to marry him, is too close to permit scepticism. To take a second example, Miss Brontë's companions at home were her sisters Emily and Anne and the servant Tabby – and Rivers' household in the novel was completed by his two sisters and an elderly servant. But the most obvious identity between fact and fiction was the name Eyre: that of a famous old Hathersage family who at one time occupied both the houses that served as models for the Marsh End or Moor House (both names were used) of the novel. There was even a real Jane Eyre. She lived at Shatton Hall, two miles along the valley from Hathersage, and married a John Thornhill of Thornhill. We can be forgiven our confusion with the fictional Jane Eyre's romance with the master of Thornfield Hall.

The novel's references to local industries faithfully reflect the Hathersage of Miss Brontë's day. So do the graphic descriptions of the scenery during Jane Eyre's desperate wanderings on the moors before she found sanctuary with the Rivers. When she fled from Mr Rochester and Thornfield Hall she travelled by coach as far as Whitcross. This has been identified as Moscar Cross, a pillar that used to stand about a third of a mile west of the existing house of the same name (between the A57 and Strines Reservoir). The old Moscar Cross was the junction of two coaching roads that have since vanished with hardly a trace. The east–west route from Sheffield to Manchester crossed the north–south highway from Yorkshire to Derbyshire: the one presumably used by Miss Brontë and her heroine. Yet every time I read the novel and try to correlate fact with fiction it seems that Fox House might also have served as Whitcross, though there is no reference to the house that already stood there in Miss Brontë's year. We have to remember, of course, that she was writing a novel, not a touring guide. In describing people and places she was blending a variety of source material – mixing her colours, so to speak.

It is evident, for example, that the Marsh End or Moor House of the book combines characteristics of two of the houses Miss Brontë came to know during her stay in Hathersage. Moorseats – partly thirteenth century but essentially built in 1682, and much changed since Miss Brontë's visit – most closely corresponds (or did) with Jane Eyre's detailed description of the house and its immediate environment. But in terms of siting, if not structure, a stronger candidate is North Lees Hall, between Moorseats and Stanage Edge. Rebuilt from 1594 to 1596, North Lees Hall is unique among Peak District manor houses because it has a romantic tower block that would look more at home in the Border Country. It could have given Miss Brontë a few ideas for Thornfield Hall, as well as Marsh End. Near by are the ruins of a small Roman Catholic chapel – built by Robert Eyre in 1685 but destroyed by a Protestant mob three years later – which was connected to the Hall by an underground passage. North Lees Hall has wide views and stands on the edge of the ancient township of Outseats, a high, mostly level wilderness that looks much the same now as it did when the turnpike road was carved across it in 1777.

Anyway, read *Jane Eyre* again. Think of Charlotte Brontë strolling about Hathersage with Ellen Nussey in 1845 and making notes. Equate Hathersage with Morton, Miss Brontë with Jane Eyre, and Henry Nussey with St John Rivers. And take it from there.

It has been claimed that the Eyres came over with William the Conqueror and that one of them fought at Hastings at the cost of a leg, was granted land in the Hope Valley, and founded a prolific family who served as wardens in the royal forest, married well, and came to own almost every big house in the valley. One descendant was a Robert Eyre who lived at Highlow Hall and installed his seven sons (some say eleven) in properties that were all within sight, keeping in touch by using a signalling system with a separate code for every house. Moving clockwise, these houses could have been Offerton, Upper and Nether Shatton, Crookhill (overlooking what is now the Ladybower Reservoir), North Lees, Moorseats and Hazelford. In the church at Hathersage is a memorial to the Robert and Joan Eyre who lived at Padley and had fourteen children. He is reputed to have been a murderer who was pardoned because of his gallantry while leading a company of archers from the Hope Valley area at the Battle of Agincourt.

Hathersage has had a church since the twelfth century and much of the present structure dates from the fourteenth or fifteenth. The porch has battlements. A chancel window was rescued from the church at Derwent before this was submerged by the Ladybower Reservoir. Centuries earlier, when there was no consecrated ground at Derwent or Bamford, their dead were transported to Hathersage on farm wagons along narrow, undulating lanes. Near the church, on the way up to Moorseats, is Camp Green, a swelling circular earthwork that probably dates from the ninth century. But the site of the oldest settlement here is at Hathersage Booths on the road that climbs to 'The Surprise'.

Hathersage had an iron-working industry in the sixteenth century and later produced buttons. At the time of Charlotte Brontë's visit employment was largely connected with wire-drawing and millstone-making. Wintry weather put the millstone-makers out of work for two or three months, but wives and children helped out by gathering blackberries and bilberries and selling them at Sheffield. Wire-drawing concerned the manufacture of needles, hackle pins, sieves (one of their functions was sorting out the lead ore), and umbrella frames.

Samuel Fox of Bradwell was connected with the Hathersage umbrella business in those days. Joseph Sheldon, born in Hathersage two months after Miss Brontë's stay, was later to recall a childhood in which he was sent to Longshaw Lodge with a big basin to beg for dripping when the Duke of Rutland was installed for the grouse-shooting season. He became a farm labourer and, via a hiring fair at Hope, moved to Stocksbridge and later worked about the house for Fox and his wife (she taught Sheldon to read and write). Sheldon then became an apprentice engineer and made rapid progress because he had a natural talent for the job and some bright ideas. When he retired on his savings (plus royalties from his inventions) he travelled the world but never lost his enthusiasm for walking – particularly to his old haunts in Hathersage, fifteen miles away. It did him no harm. He was a month short of his 90th birthday when he died at Stocksbridge.

Hathersage, formerly Hathersitch and still similarly

pronounced Hathersidge, is beautifully located – and best viewed from the Highlow area across the valley. It has a gala in July, has become a popular home address for people who work in Sheffield, and has congenial hotels in the Hathersage Inn and the George. I came out of the George one morning and saw two ladies vigorously cleaning the glass in the telephone box across the road, which seemed an odd thing to be doing – especially on a Sunday. The road, as usual, was busy. But a sheep casually ambled across it, then came back and wandered into the school yard. It seemed that, essentially, the pace of life had not changed much since the days of Little John, the Eyres, and Charlotte Brontë.

West of Hathersage is a road junction at the confluence of the Derwent and one of its tributaries, the Noe. This was a familiar spot to the travellers of old and used to have two tollgates and a smithy. A modern bridge was built a few yards from the old one, which itself succeeded a ford. Originally Mittenforde, then Mythomstede Bridge, today's Mythom Bridge has three alternative spellings. It is not mentioned on either of my maps, so presumably the cartographers gave up on it.

Bamford has no history of any consequence before the last 200 years or so. The old ford is supposed to lie below the weir – made of gritstone from Bamford Edge – that was built to serve the mill on which Bamford's development was based. Formerly a corn mill, this was converted to cotton-spinning and remained in the textile business until 1965. Its owners were a Manchester family firm, cotton doublers and manufacturers of lace thread. The big noise in the nineteenth century was William Cameron Moore, one of the partners at the mill, an important landowner who was chiefly responsible for endowing the church (1860) and building the vicarage (1863). The Moores had already given Bamford the benefit of the mill, cottages for the workers, and a school – where services were held until the church was completed (the Wesleyans had got in first with a chapel built in 1821).

In all this there is an echo of Arkwright's Cromford. Local legend has it that W. C. Moore ruined himself by keeping the mill going during the slump, to prevent unemployment.

These days one of Bamford's most obvious features is the relatively modern estate of fifty-four stone houses built up the road to accommodate families evacuated from the villages of Ashopton and Derwent. What a terrible experience it must have been to see your home demolished, then drowned by a reservoir – and go to live within a mile or so of the memories. Mod cons may ease heartache but cannot cure it. This estate is near Yorkshire Bridge. The bridge itself produced an odd incident when, during its construction, a toad was found entombed in a hole in a coping-stone.

On each spring bank holiday Monday the recreation ground at Bamford is enlivened by sheepdog trials, a sheep-shearing contest, and a well-dressing exhibition; and for a week in July the village street is gaily decorated for the annual carnival. Up the slopes behind the gritstone houses you may spot a sparrowhawk perched watchfully on a crag and planning a rather messy carnival of its own. Bamford has an attractive setting: the broad Derwent valley is almost surrounded by the bulky heights of Bamford Edge, Win Hill, and (more distantly) Derwent Edge and Offerton Moor.

Win Hill and its western neighbour Lose Hill probably took their names from 'wind' and 'loose' (which in any case is the correct pronunciation for Lose Hill). But a combination of word-association, speculation, history and legend has inevitably come up with a more interesting theory. This concerns a series of battles between two rival kings, Edwin of Northumbria and Penda of Mercia, in 632. An alternative version puts Edwin in the ring with King Cuicholm of Wessex. Anyway, the winning army (Penda beat Edwin but Edwin beat Cuicholm) camped on Win Hill and the losers camped across the way.

At 1,516ft the twin peaks of Win Hill are always breezy but command views that in their variety and grandeur are

unsurpassed in the Peak District – the cool blue of Ladybower
Reservoir, the greenness of the valleys and the hills draped
with woods, and distant high moorlands that somehow pack
a great range of hues into a basic brown. Win Hill has most
of the qualities of a genuine mountain. It stands in lofty
isolation except for a narrow ridge that transforms it into a
wedge-shaped tail of the Kinder Scout massif. There are
times when that ridge seems like the roof of the world.
About thirty years ago I was up there with my brother at
dusk, making for Hope at the end of a tiring day, when the
soft curtain of mist suddenly lifted and way down in the east
we saw the ghostly stump of Derwent's church tower rising
from the drought-lowered waters of Ladybower. The memory
is as chilling now as the vision was then. That ridge can be an
eerie place. It is crossed by an old British track that was used
by the Romans as a link between Anavio (Brough) and
Melandra, near Glossop, and legend has it that the spirits of
the Roman legions are still marching. That sounds ridiculous.
But get yourself up on that ridge and walk down to Fullwood
Stile Farm, just outside Hope, while the light is fading. You
may be alone – but it will not feel that way.

Win Hill is a lot of yesterdays. Cooking in the rain while
camping at Twitchill Farm. Watching, incredulously, as the
farmer castrated lambs with his teeth. The look on ramblers'
faces as the world squash rackets champion, Jonah Barring-
ton, jogged past them up the hill in a spectral white track suit
and, on the summit, threw himself into a vigorous series of
press-ups. Ebenezer Elliott (1781–1849), the 'Corn-Law
Rhymer', was much more deferential when – at a time when
such heights were still mysterious, because relatively un-
explored – he inspected the giant's most impressive aspect
from the vicinity of the Ladybower Inn. His address to Win
Hill was, with every respect to both, a little effusive ('Star-
loved, and meteor-sought, and tempest-found! Proud centre
of a mountain-circle, hail!'). Never mind. He was a good man.
Descended from cattle thieves in the Border Country,

Elliott was a nature-lover who became a master-founder at Sheffield and was active in literature and politics. He was the poet of the poor and bitterly condemned the bread tax – which obsessed him – in verses known as the *Corn-Law Rhymes*. In spite of his relentlessly fiery zeal when inspired by a sense of injustice, Elliott was a small, meek-looking chap. When he died the working men of Sheffield paid for a bronze statue, which sits on a rock in Weston Park.

Lose Hill, 1,563ft, is the eastern peak of a spectacular ridge. The top has been National Trust property since 1945 in memory of G. H. B. Ward, a Sheffield man who fought tenaciously for public rights of way over moorland the landowners wanted to reserve for grouse and those who shoot them. Elliott would have liked his style. In 1948 the summit of Lose Hill acquired Derbyshire's first view-finder, a circular bronze plaque indicating the contours and seventy-three features. Down the southern slopes is Losehill Hall, a modernised Victorian mansion set in twenty-seven acres of parkland. Opened by the national-park authority in 1972, this residential study centre offers a wide range of courses concerning the Peak District.

Hope, dominated from a respectful distance by the twin bulks of Win Hill and Lose Hill, is a junction of roads and rivers and has a rare historic importance reflected to some extent in its continuing status as the heart of the Hope Valley – which is the heart of the Peak District as a whole. It also has a well-dressing and wakes festival and, on August bank holiday Monday, sheepdog trials and an agricultural show. But in spite of all this Hope remains more of a request stop than a terminus, more of a working village and dormitory than a tourist attraction in itself. Visitors pass through on their way to Castleton, Edale or the surrounding heights and at the end of the day they pass through again in the opposite direction. *Sic transit gloria mundi.* So passes away the glory of the world. But that is Hope's story, too. The village has seen it all and now sits back and lets the world go by.

Anavio was less than a mile away and a Roman road passed south of Hope's present church. The settlement itself was Saxon: tenth century or earlier. Before the Norman conquest it was already the heart of a parish that, though thinly populated, was one of the largest in England: flanked by the Derwent in the east, the Glossop-to-Buxton area in the west, and occupying about two-thirds of the Peak Forest. In a field behind the Woodroffe Arms, near the church, there once stood an early Norman castle, a modest structure of earth and wood. A branch of the Eyre family used to live opposite the church at the Old Hall, now an inn. And as we remember from Joseph Sheldon's story, Hope used to have a hiring fair. In short, the village is very much more than a name on the map, a bend on the road. It has done a lot of living: which reminds me that, as children, we soon became familiar with our elders' philosophic joke 'We must live in Hope even if we die in Castleton'.

During the Napoleonic Wars every parish had to produce a fixed number of fighting men and when lots were drawn in Hope Church there was a riot. Miners from such places as Castleton, Bradwell, Tideswell, Eyam and Longstone marched on Bakewell (where the justices were sitting) armed with picks, shovels, and a variety of other makeshift weapons – and made a bonfire of their call-up papers. When redirected, the same sort of spirit made awful dents in Napoleon's dignity.

Near the south porch of the church is the shaft of a ninth- or tenth-century cross that was restored to once piece after being found in two – built into the walls of the old school. Over the porch is a turreted room. The church itself, probably built on the site of its Saxon predecessor, is chiefly fourteenth and fifteenth century. It contains two coffin slabs carved to represent crosses and forestry implements, suggesting that the slabs originally marked foresters' graves. St Peter's also has an extraordinary collection of vestments, documents, and plate – so valuable that it is only given an airing during the well-dressing festival and at Easter and Christmas.

The traditional verbal warfare exchanged between the villages insists that whereas the natives of Bradwell are the descendants of slave labour imported by the Romans, the original inhabitants of Castleton were the home-grown equivalent: aboriginals who had to do the dirty work for the Romans and other invaders. Nowadays Castleton is a tourist attraction because of its caverns, Blue John stone, the vestiges of Peveril Castle, and the dramatic grandeur of a valley-end environment dominated by Mam Tor, the 'Shivering Mountain'. It is also the Peak District's best example of a medieval village of this size, though the tourist traffic sometimes makes the fact difficult to appreciate. But Castleton never developed the independent importance suggested by its geographical advantages, its historic association with lead mines and trading routes, and the care with which the village was laid out by the 'town planners' of the twelfth century. The place did not even expand to the boundaries the Normans set for it.

After Edward the Confessor had done the ground work William the Conqueror firmly imposed the feudal system. He crushed Saxon resistance, transferred most of the land to Normans, built castles, replaced Saxon by Norman clergy, insisted that everybody's first loyalty was to the king, and to aid his tax collectors swiftly completed the Domesday survey of lands, values and population. As his top man in the Peak District he appointed his bastard son and favourite, William Peveril, to serve as bailiff of the royal forest – including its lead mines. Peveril's son was to be disinherited in 1155 for poisoning his mistress's husband, the Earl of Chester. But that did not affect the development of the Norman 'new town' at Castleton. This, and the royal forest as a whole, was governed from Peveril Castle, which dominated the settlement from a commanding height between the steep drops to Cave Dale and the Peak Cavern. There was a castle on this natural fortress before the Conquest but it was rebuilt between 1175 and 1177. Its great period was from the twelfth to the fourteenth centuries, though its use as a royal hunting lodge carried over into the fifteenth. The guests at Peveril Castle included three kings: Henry II, Henry III and Edward III. By the seventeenth century the place was in ruins and there is little left now except for the shell of the keep built in 1176: the Peak District's only substantial relic of a Norman castle. The keep originally had two storeys and a basement connected by a spiral staircase set into walls 8ft thick. In 1403 the castle ceased to be the base of noblemen controlling the royal forest, but the keep was later used as a prison and there is a gruesome tradition that walled-up bones were discovered near the staircase. In 1823 Sir Walter Scott's *Peveril of the Peak* was to give the castle fictional renown and revive interest in its history.

Half a mile west of Castleton the Hope Valley ends abruptly at a hill called Treak Cliff, one of the Peak District's most remarkable repositories of marine fossils – and the world's only known source of the attractively banded fluorspar called Blue John. The name may have been a corruption of *bleu-jaune* (the French were among the first to put the stone to ornamental use) or a miners' nickname to distinguish it from the zinc blende known as Black Jack. Fluorspar is usually white or cream – but blue, purple, black and yellow are all found in the brittle and crystalline Blue John, a difficult stone to work. It was discovered in the seventeenth century and first adapted for decorative purposes in the eighteenth, notably by Henry Watson, whom we met at Ashford in the Water. But some local publicists try to kid themselves and the tourists that two Blue John vases were discovered when Pompeii was excavated and that, consequently, the stone must have been worked at Castleton in Roman times. The legend is explained by the fact that the Romans imported a similar mineral from Iran.

The Tazza Vase at Chatsworth is probably the largest object made from Blue John, which was formerly widely used for vases and inlays. Nowadays the supply is limited but you will find plenty of trinkets in the shops of Castleton. Treak Cliff is riddled with lead-mine workings and natural caverns rich in the cool, graceful beauty of stalactites and stalagmites. Blue John has been worked in the now abandoned Old Tor Mine (between the Treak Cliff Cavern and Winnats Pass) and in the two subterranean tourist attractions, the Blue John Cavern and the Treak Cliff Cavern. Some of the loveliest lime formations are in caves discovered by miners as recently as 1926. Three years earlier miners had broken into another cave and made a less welcome find: Bronze Age skeletons.

Castleton's two other 'show' caverns are awesome. This is particularly true of the Peak Cavern's vast entrance, 60ft high and 100ft wide, which gapes from the foot of the dark, mighty precipice soaring to the keep of Peveril Castle. The sight is so daunting that its traditional associations are easy to understand. Until the nineteenth century even formal guidebooks knew the Peak Cavern as the Devil's Arse. When heavy rain flooded the cavern the Devil was said to be relieving himself, and the stream by the main path was named after the mythological 'river of hate', the Styx, which flowed round Hades. Peakshole Water, which joins the Noe at Hope, issues from the mouth of the cavern, where long terraces have been cut into the limestone. These rope-walks (ropes were needed for mining) were used from the fifteenth or sixteenth century until well into the twentieth and on the roof of the cavern, just inside the entrance, are areas darkened by smoke from the chimneys of vanished houses that accommodated the rope-makers and their families. Passages wind into the hill for a mile and one of the series of caverns measures 150ft by 90ft by 60ft. The temperature remains constant at 47°F.

The Speedwell Cavern, at the foot of Winnats Pass, is approached via more than a hundred steps. It was a failure as a lead mine but swiftly became a success with tourists. Remember James Brindley's boat-haulage of coal through that

These photographs, taken from opposite directions over Ladybower reservoir, are poignant reminders of the drowned village of Derwent. The war memorial was moved before its original location – near the anglers in the picture below – was submerged

(*above*) What looks like a ruined fortress is in fact The Tower, which was slowly eroded and detached from Alport Castles, the cliff on the right. This astonishing landslip lies in one of the Peak District's most secluded dales; (*below*) on the way from Derwent Dale to Alport Castles. But the scene is so typical that it could simply be captioned 'Walking in the Peak District'

1761 tunnel at Worsley? The same idea was applied here for getting lead out. Between 1774 and 1781 a half-mile, circular tunnel was bored and then half-filled with water diverted from the caves. Tourists still use boats – traditionally propelled either by 'legging' (lying on your back and pushing on the roof with your feet) or by manhandling pegs driven into the walls. Your reward for the ordeal by steps and tunnel is to stand on a platform across a huge and horrific vertical cavern that drops 70ft below tunnel level and soars upwards into distant darkness. Like Eldon Hole this was formerly known as the Bottomless Pit. The children may love it. Father may be impressed. Mother may wish she had waited outside.

Other than the tourist caverns, we should note a further series of mine workings and natural cavities that stretch for three-quarters of a mile under Mam Tor. These used to be the Odin Mine, traditionally associated with the Danes, though there is no evidence that it was worked until the seventeenth century. The ore was unusually rich but the flooding unusually heavy and persistent. The mine was closed in 1847 but below the road and the mine entrance are a crushing wheel and a circular iron track, the relics of a horse-gin used to diminish the lead ore. Once upon a time a local man saw firelight in a small cave at the entrance. Curiosity was swiftly succeeded by panic when he discovered a stranger sharing the warmth of the fire with a huge bear. In the old days bears were taken round the fairs, but it must have been a little disturbing to meet one in a cave.

As you have gathered, the great semi-circle of hills that form the western terminus of the Hope Valley is to some extent hollow, with water sloshing about everywhere. This may be interesting for tourists, potholers, cavers, and other explorers, but in conjunction with landslips – in addition to limestone and gritstone, the earth's crust hereabouts has bands of more friable shales – it has had an astonishing effect on Mam Tor and the A625, which may now have been closed for good. Nature designed Castleton as a dead-end village and seems to be insisting on it. The road built in 1820 and rebuilt by prisoners of war in the 1940s weaves across a hillside that always seems to be slipping, dipping and twisting this way and that. Mam Tor is a restless reminder of the natural forces that created this landscape in the first place. The outside edge of the road tends to sag and crack and fall away as if at the mercy of a quietly insidious earthquake. When I was there in 1979 the A625 was an awful sight, the rumbling flow of heavy traffic had ceased, motorists could no longer reach the Blue John Cavern by the direct route from Castleton, and Man seemed to have given up the fight with powers beyond his control.

The 1,695ft Mam Tor, which may commemorate a pagan mother goddess, is a crumbling giant known as the 'Shivering Mountain'. The steep southern face, sheared away by erosive landslips, is vastly spectacular. But the tumbling detritus launched a flanking attack on that ill-fated road and also removed a section of Mam Tor's hill fort, the largest in the Peak District. The camp had double ramparts and supposedly overlapped the Bronze and Iron Ages. It is a windy spot commanding an extensive panorama and the ridge walk to Lose Hill can be recommended. Note the hillocks and hollows indicating further landslips on the northern slopes of Mam Tor and Back Tor.

Castleton's garlanding ceremony, usually held on the evening of 29 May (Oak Apple Day), may be derived from a pagan May Day ritual and in its modern form dates from 1749 or even earlier. Its theme is the legend that Charles II hid in an oak tree after his defeat at Worcester in 1651. A 'king' and 'lady' in seventeenth-century Stuart costumes lead a procession from the Nag's Head to Castleton's five other pubs and eventually the church. The 'king's' head and shoulders are encased in a heavy garland of leaves and flowers constructed on a conical framework and at the church this is rope-hauled to the top of the tower and left there until the flowers wither. You could describe the whole thing as a fancy-dress pub crawl complete with music and dancing.

At the Nag's Head one evening my wife and I were served with a special Derbyshire hors d'oeuvre: Yorkshire pudding with onion sauce and gravy. Yorkshire pudding is commonly associated with roast beef but in the North it is also used as a dessert (with jam) and, less often, as a hors d'oeuvre. In the bar I met one of those quiet, reflective men who spend most of their time in open country with only the wind and the sheep for company. He talked to me about dry-stone walling and said it was like doing a jigsaw: you were always looking for the right piece and never picked up a stone until you had a place for it. It seems he had given up farm work for an unusual reason: 'T' boss were climbing over a stile wi' a gun in 'is 'and, and blew 'is 'ead off.' Our companions in that cosy old coaching inn were persuaded to discuss the problems of living in a tourist village in a national park. They thought many of the restrictions imposed on residents were petty. They resented the fact that old cottages were bought at high prices for weekend use by outsiders. As for visitors, the worst problems were litter ('They just chuck it over the wall – we're always clearing it out of the garden'); the often inadequate supervision of school parties among the hazards of cliffs and open mine shafts; and the way some groups of walkers ignored traffic and wandered about the roads like sheep.

There is much more we could say about Castleton: about the church's Norman chancel arch and ancient oak pews; the market place, which diminished as the churchyard expanded; and the crude pottery, stone hammer and bronze axe that ancient man left behind in the recesses of Cave Dale. And of course there is 'Wind Gates', the renowned Winnats Pass, a steep and narrow gorge that can be a desperately nasty place when the snow lies deep and the wind is howling. How travellers of old must have welcomed the ringing comfort of Castleton's 7 pm curfew. The rock-strewn Winnats route has always been tricky but has frequently served as a necessary alternative to Mam Tor. In 1757 the horse and packhorse traffic began to give way to cumbersome coaches on the new turnpike from Sheffield to Ringinglow, Winnats, Chapel-en-le-Frith and Manchester. In 1820 the turnpike up Winnats was deprived of its main function, or so they thought, by the new road up Mam Tor. But we know what happened to that.

Winnats is supposedly haunted by the ghosts of two run-away lovers, Clara and Henry (Allan, in another version of the story). On their way to Peak Forest and marriage in 1758 they stopped at a Castleton inn to refresh themselves and check the route. The conversation was overheard by five miners who noted the couple's obvious wealth and slipped out quietly to wait for them up Winnats. Henry was murdered with a pick, Clara by means unrecorded. The bodies were thrown down a cavity in the vicinity of what later became the Speedwell Mine, and the riderless horses galloped into Sparrowpit. The story did not end there. The bodies were discovered ten years later during the construction of a mine shaft. The killers were never caught but one made a deathbed confession after a long illness. The others, it seems, had died in nasty, retributive circumstances. Near the scene of the crime, one had a fatal fall and another was crushed by tumbling rock. A third went mad and the fourth hanged himself. It has, alternatively, been alleged that one perished in a thunderstorm. But accounts differ only on points of detail. It is said that when the whining wind is lashing Winnats you can still hear Clara and Henry begging for mercy.

In 1978 a cavern as big as Sheffield Cathedral was discovered under Winnats. At the head of the pass is Windy Knoll, where rhinoceros, bear, and wolf bones were found in a cave. Just to the west is Giant's Hole, almost 500ft deep, one of Britain's deepest potholes: about two miles of passages and caves have been explored and there may be more to come.

To the north, on Rushup Edge, is a Bronze Age burial mound known as Lord's Seat. The eastern extension of this same ridge used to be traversed – at Hollins Cross, a view-point beyond Mam Tor – by a coffin track. Until their first chapel was consecrated in 1634 the people of Edale had to go to Castleton for worship or burial. As if the trip itself was not enough of an imposition for the faithful (especially when sharing the company of the coffined dead) they had to pass a lazaretto – a hospital for those with contagious diseases – situated near the point where the track to Losehill Hall now joins the A625. As a result of this transient proximity the Edale folk had to use the same 'Devil's entrance' to the churchyard and the church as the unfortunates from the lazaretto – many of whom had to stay outside and listen to the service from a safe distance (safe, that is, for everybody else).

Edale is now better organised. The present church is the third in the village and has a lovely setting. So has every-thing else in Edale, for that matter: including mountain rescue and national park information centres, camping sites and ski runs (the latter opened in 1960), and a seventeenth-century corn mill that later served the tanning and textile trades and was recently converted into flats. A century ago this bustling recreational activity would have been unthinkable, because the broad valley of Edale is almost surrounded by the stern heights of the Kinder Scout massif and that long ridge from Lose Hill to Rushup Edge. The Noe just manages to weave through to Hope, but there is not much of a gap at Edale End (where a woman was frozen to death in 1711). It does not take much imagination to envisage this secret dale as a miniaturised equivalent of the Lötschen Tal, a branch of the Rhone Valley so isolated among mountains that medieval customs survived for centuries.

Edale might have kept the world at bay a little longer but for the railway opened in 1894, which ducks into the Cowburn Tunnel at Barber Booth, and the creation of the Pennine Way between 1951 and 1965. But when the walkers, climbers, campers and trippers discovered Edale and Kinder Scout, Fred Heardman taught them how to enjoy and respect what they found. In 1931 this remarkable man bought two inns. He held both licences for fifteen years before selling the Church Inn and settling at the Nag's Head, where he combined the functions of innkeeper, rambler, information officer, warden, mountain rescue organiser and museum curator. Heardman had a great affection for the Peak District and opened windows in the minds of all who knew him.

Edale appeared in the Domesday Book as 'Aidele' and has had at least five other spellings. All of them applied to the valley rather than the village, which consisted merely of Grindsbrook Booth (the 'i' pronounced as in mind or rind). Booths were farm holdings on land that was enclosed to keep out wolves and the five at Edale – Upper, Barber, Grindsbrook, Ollerbrook and Nether Booths – were originally rented from the Crown by foresters or private landowners.

The tide of tourism floods through Edale without doing much harm. Best viewed from the ridge to the south, Edale is the popular approach to the bleak moorland of Kinder Scout and the beginning or the end of many strenuously superb walks. The biggest of these, of course, is the 250-mile Pennine Way to Kirk Yetholm in Scotland. Either of the two official routes out of Edale – via Grindsbrook or Upper Booth – will swiftly give you two samples of what to expect. One is the ascent, the other is an expanse of featureless peat bog marked on the map as 'Pennine Way undefined'. The Upper Booth route goes by way of a packhorse bridge and Jacob's Ladder, a steep, grassy slope where an eighteenth-century tradesman called Jacob Marshall hacked out some steps so that he could take a short cut while his pony went along the lane. Generations of ramblers have made such a mess of the slope that the 'ladder' is now more of a slide. There are plenty of well-worn packhorse routes round Edale and one of these, at the eastern end of Kinder, has left a telling name on the map: Jaggers Clough, which rises from Edale End. Jaggers were the men who led the packhorse trains.

Kinder Scout is a dull, dangerous, exhilarating wilderness. A plateau that covers five square miles and rises to a maximum height of 2,088ft between the Downfall and Crowden Tower, which makes it the flattest but highest 'peak' in the Peak District. A dirty, featureless desert that somehow got stuck up in the clouds and the rain and soaked up all the wetness. An empty mass of peat hags (banks) and groughs (drainage channels, pronounced 'gruffs'). A brown, clinging morass that looks as if it has been used as a midden since the beginning of time. The groughs can be sticky after rain, the bogs even more so. Route-finding can be nerve-wracking – and impossible in mist (use your compass and get down fast). The mucky terrain is too familiar to mountain rescue teams and not familiar enough to most other bog-trotters. In short, Kinder Scout is bad news.

Do I tempt you? Of course I do, because you realise that these are the censorious insults that spring from a reluctant affection – plus an insistence that you should treat the thrilling, silent world of Kinder Scout with the utmost respect.

The 'i' in Kinder, by the way, is pronounced as in kith and kin. The name is thought to be an adaptation of Kyndwr Scut, meaning water over the edge. Let us dash round (easier written than done) a few of the names on the map, working clockwise from Edale. Edale Head is a great bowl among crags. Edale Cross, probably twelfth century but dated 1610, is an old boundary marker and travellers' guide that lay broken on the ground until it was re-erected in 1810 by local farmers (one, John Gee, put his initials on it). Kinder Low is a triangulation pillar at 2,077ft, half a mile south-west of the 'peak', which is 11ft higher. Cluther Rocks (it means 'cluster') are among many oddly shaped outcrops on Kinder. William Clough is so called because 'William the Smith' smelted iron there in the thirteenth century. Featherbed Moss, near the A57, is one of several areas given this name because of the abundance of fluffy white cotton grass. Fairbrook Naze is the eastern extremity of The Edge, Kinder's northern rampart.

And the Seal Stones do look rather like seals, though the word is so common in this vicinity that it might have been derived from the sallow (mountain willow), formerly 'sealh'.

Kinder Downfall demands more attention because it is the only large waterfall in the Peak District and has some strange characteristics. Its winter drapery of icicles is an astonishing sight. In summer the Downfall almost ceases to exist and at other times, given a strong flow of water and a boisterous westerly wind, a great deal of it is blown upwards – so far beyond the point of departure that the cloud of spray can soak anyone standing within 100 yards of the top. You have to be lucky to see this phenomenon but my brother and I did so while the early chapters of this book were being written. We sauntered up from the Snake Inn at a pace that made due allowance for middle age. It was good to see again the peat-brown water of those moorland brooks. The scattered wreckage of a light aircraft was a reminder of many wartime crashes on Kinder and the surrounding heights. And then we were on the top, approaching the Downfall – and suddenly, distantly, it seemed that nature's kettle was on the boil or that someone had just lit a garden fire. The wind was the kind that grabs you and shakes you and, in the absence of any human substitute for roots, threatens to toss you about from place to place. Standing at the top of the Downfall was like being in a heavy shower that was rising – yes, rising – sideways. One got wet from the pockets upwards.

The top of the Downfall is a wasteland of water and peat hags and sandstone, and the junction of the two Pennine Way routes from Edale. The River Kinder, a modest but attractive moorland stream in summer, approaches its 100ft plunge via a jungle of boulders and a few pretty pools in which it pauses as if getting up courage. Then it drops, leaping into space from ledge to ledge – or trying to. But a fierce wind can hurl it back whence it came and way up into the sky. What does it is the presence of two converging cliffs that concentrate the fury of the wind in the angle formed between them.

Anyway, after seeing that waterfall going upwards, we exchanged no more than a glance when we were passed by a cyclist.

Below the Downfall is the Mermaid's Pool. The lady is supposed to come up for a swim and a look round during Easter weekend and it is said that if you see her you will live for ever. The chances of doing either are not good. Kinder Reservoir, lower down, would be an arresting sight from above if closely framed by trees. At its south-eastern extremity is Upper House, where Mary Augusta Arnold (1851–1920), better known as Mrs Humphry Ward, wrote much of *The History of David Grieve*, setting the early scenes among these same moors. The grand-daughter of Thomas Arnold of Rugby and niece of Matthew Arnold, the poet, she wrote twenty-three novels based on the people she knew, the opinions she held, and the problems of the day. One of the opinions was that women should not be granted the right to vote.

Kinder Scout is extraordinary: high, wide, and in its own way, handsome. Granted two sound legs and a taste for bog-trotting, there is no finer walk in the Peak District than the round tour. You can slice off samples between Hayfield and the Snake Inn, via William Clough, or between Hayfield and Edale via Edale Cross. But this is no place for a Sunday afternoon stroll. So do your homework, dress for the job, and pack a compass and torch – the last in case a rescue team has to find you.

7
The Longdendale Ghosts

FROM BLEAKLOW AND LONGDENDALE TO DERWENT DALE
AND BRADFIELD
See map pages 204–205

For all the physical and emotional stress it imposes, Kinder Scout does inspire a certain warmth of regard. It does not drain all the laughter out of living. The wilderness contrasts sharply with the civilised world but keeps in touch – except on its northern flank. No one jokes much about Bleaklow and Black Hill, except in a sour way. Longdendale, the largest of the three wards in the old royal forest, was described in the Domesday survey as 'waste'. It has not changed much, in spite of the man-made mess in the valley of the Etherow. This is land at the end of its tether. The brooding emptiness of the moors is chilling, harsh, hostile. Nature is totally, ruthlessly in control. Emily Brontë and Thomas Hardy might have been responsive to the personality of Longdendale (the old ward, as distinct from the valley of the same name) but most of us confront its desolate challenges only because of the perverse determination that makes a man measure himself against natural hazards. The terrain makes walking tough, slow, exhausting. The weather can change rapidly from sunshine to thick, swirling mist. The threat of death by exposure never recedes far. So precautions are necessary. Like checking the local weather forecast and leaving behind a note of your planned route. Like preparing for emergencies by packing a torch, whistle and first-aid kit. Like ensuring that a map and compass are in the pockets and healthy food and a hot drink in the rucksack. Like wearing warm, weatherproof clothing and strong, comfortable boots. Because this is serious business.

Kinder Scout and Bleaklow are separated by the A57 and what is popularly known as the Snake Pass. This is a spectacular drive with views of breathtaking grandeur, especially on the west-to-east run. But take care, beware of sheep, and ask your passengers to look out for hares and sparrowhawks. A few miles out of Glossop the pass reaches its summit with a straight stretch at 1,680ft, vulnerable to heavy snowfalls that often close the road. It is at this point that the Pennine Way crosses the Snake onto Bleaklow and the wildest stretch of the entire 250-mile route. Just north of the A57 the Pennine Way intersects Doctor's Gate, the course of the Roman road from Anavio to Melandra, which runs down Shelf Brook into Old Glossop. The name, it is said, is either a corruption of 'Dog Tor' or was derived from a Dr Talbot.

The A57 descends to join the River Ashop in the Woodlands Valley at the isolated Snake Inn, a welcome sight to many a tired and troubled traveller. It was built in 1821 to cater for coach traffic on the new Sheffield–Glossop road, and as the Duke of Devonshire was a major shareholder in the turnpike trust the inn took its name from the Cavendish family crest. The road in turn took its name from the inn, though the reverse is often assumed to be the case. The first landlord, John Longden, was also a farmer and Methodist preacher (Methodism quickly took root in the Woodlands, and prayer meetings were held at farms and later at the inn before the existing small chapel was built in 1868 near the confluence of the Ashop and Alport). When the road closes, the Snake Inn closes, and at the best of times their most reliable form of trade consists of what they call 'functions'. I stayed there recently, had a warm welcome and some memorable breakfasts, and gathered that a boorish minority of ramblers tended to bring the entire breed under suspicion.

Down the road, just below Hey Ridge, two Edale farmers were collecting loads of wood in 1830 when there was a sudden flood down the Woodlands Valley. Men, horses and timber were all swept away. The bodies turned up later at

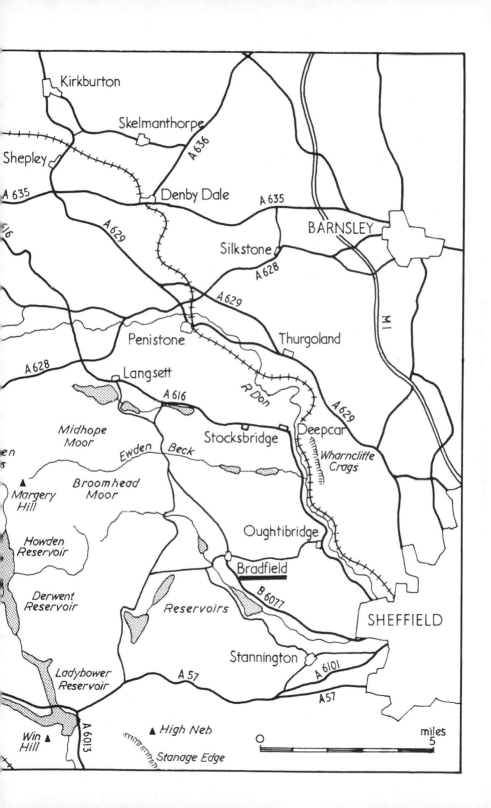

Grindleford, about twelve miles downstream. The valley gave its name to Whitefaced Woodland sheep, known as Penistones in Yorkshire because of their traditional association with Penistone's markets. Large and Roman-nosed, these sheep are the descendants of the huge monastic flocks of medieval times. It is thought that the native stock was improved when the Romans imported white-faced sheep. In the eighteenth century Merino rams from Spain enhanced the quality and quantity of the wool, which was used for making such felt products as hats.

Hagg Farm, a national-park hostel, should not be confused with the older, now deserted Bellhagg Farm, which at one time had a shop and even served as a school. Outside Bellhagg Farm is the remnant of an iron-ringed stone cheese press. Inside are the blackened shell of the chimney, birds' nests, sheep droppings, decay, and imagined echoes of many bustling yesterdays. When my brother and I popped in, there was also one obviously dead sheep; lying on its side, left ear to the floor. It had found shelter, but too late. We looked around for a while and then did an incredulous double-take at that sheep. Its head was in a different position! They say internal gases and lubricants do strange things to the body after death. But it seemed a good time to leave.

Bleaklow is from the old English 'blaec hlaw', meaning dark hill. One of the largest areas in England without a road, it has been described as the country's only true desert. There are not many tracks of any kind. Just a boggy, sepia solitude strewn with rocks, peat, heather, sphagnum and cotton grass. The rainfall is heavy, the drainage poor, the soil acid. You will see sheep and possibly the 'white' mountain hare, which changes its coat and colouring with the seasons. You may hear the curlew, meadow pipit and grouse. But there is not much to relieve the loneliness. Most of these wild, high moorlands were once reserved for grouse but public access is now restricted only in certain areas on certain days. The shooting butts and dilapidated cabins can be useful to the bog-trotter trapped in bad weather.

The two highest points, both at 2,060ft, are Bleaklow Head and, a mile and a half to the east, the strangely shaped Bleaklow Stones. In decent weather there is a particularly good view from Higher Shelf Stones at 2,038ft. Near Bleaklow Head are the Wain Stones, which from one direction look like a couple about to kiss. They lie on the route of the Pennine Way – which connects Devil's Dike, a groove that looks man-made, with Torside Castle, where there are suggestions of ancient earthworks. Devil's Dike is so close to Doctor's Gate that there has inevitably been speculation about a Roman track between the Snake Pass and Longdendale, where Roman ghost stories are unusually prevalent. But before leaving Bleaklow we should note that near Swains Greave (the source of the Derwent) there are superb views from the vicinity of the bizarre Barrow Stones and the prominent, pock-marked Grinah Stones.

The name Longdendale, once applied to a ward of the royal forest, is now used to describe the valley of the Etherow, a tributary of the Mersey. The valley was once forested and later had a string of hamlets, including the thriving communities of Crowden and Woodhead. That stretch of the Etherow between Tintwistle ('Tinsel') and Pikenaze Moor has always been dominated by the frowning moorland heights of Bleaklow and Black Hill, but it must once have had a gloomy dignity about it and perhaps a semblance of beauty. Today's Longdendale has the heavy, rumbling traffic of the A628, an ugly necklace of five reservoirs, a railway line, and electricity pylons. The stations at Crowden and Woodhead have been closed but that has merely robbed Longdendale of its vitality. The mess remains. Nature's dramatic grandeur has been ravaged and the communities have contracted and almost died. Crowden, for example, used to have shops, a school, a pub and a mansion. Thanks to the 1965 conversion of a row of cottages, it now has a youth hostel, a café, a mountain rescue post, and an open-air-pursuits centre. Crowden, in short, serves the needs of those seeking the loneliness of high places.

Odd happenings have been reported for centuries in this brooding, introverted valley – and the stories have recently become persistent. They concern Roman ghosts, Satanism, strange lights on the moors, a disembodied voice shouting to attract attention, the sudden apparition of a black wall across an open road, and the frightening sequel to a bomber crash.

The Romans are not thought to have bothered much with Longdendale but they were definitely in the area and had battles with local Brigantes. They could have had a track over Bleaklow and some sort of fort at Torside Castle. Legend says the soldiers still appear at the first full moon in spring but what is more to the point is a series of recent reports from people who claim to have seen two or three Roman soldiers. The slightly disturbing logic about these reports – reflected in similar reports from that eerie track on Win Hill – is that the ghosts were visible only from the knees upwards. That makes a kind of sense: because the Roman tracks were at a lower level and have since been overlaid. One lady told me that while out on the moors one day she repeatedly heard a loud, unusual noise ('like knives and forks clanking in a tin box') but in spite of a diligent search could find no source for it. When she told others about the incident they said 'Oh, you've heard it too'. The noise was supposedly the clanking armour and swords of the Romans.

Half a mile from Crowden, perched up a bank between the A628 and the moors, is Woodhead's dark, small, simple church. In the churchyard are the overgrown graves of some of the navvies killed during the construction of the first Woodhead railway tunnel. The church and churchyard have both been vandalised and the church desecrated by self-styled Satanists. Rumours of naked witches whooping it up on the moors were presumably a deprecatory embellishment that quickly acquired no-smoke-without-fire stature. Any woman cavorting about Longdendale naked would swiftly find herself in an intensive care unit.

The ghost stories are fun in their way, the Satanism appalling. Those lights on the moors, though, defy a totally satisfying explanation. There are two kinds. One is a single powerful beam – rather like a searchlight or the combined headlights of a distant car approaching the brow of a hill – that has been seen in the vicinity of Bramah Edge and Clough Edge, beyond Torside Reservoir, but never advances beyond the high rim of moorland. The other is a string of moving, elusive, and eventually fading lights that often appear on the remote, craggy heights of Bleaklow beyond Shining Clough. Rescue teams have turned out, because ramblers on these desolate moors are advised to carry torches for emergency use. But no one was ever found – nor, indeed, any clue to the source of those lights.

A pilot tells me that Bleaklow is the logical approach to Ringway and the approximate area in which landing lights would be switched on. Such lights could appear suddenly over the side of a hill or while an aircraft was turning. Most civil aircraft using Ringway would have between two and six landing lights. A single beam suggested a smaller aircraft. Reports of a wandering string of lights were less easily explained. They could not be an aircraft's cabin lights because if these were close enough to be seen clearly they would be accompanied by the noise of the aircraft. Could the cause be methane, otherwise known as marsh gas or fire-damp, which is released by decaying vegetation and can be inflammable when mixed with air? Perhaps. But it is doubtful if such an explanation would have escaped the attention of the rescue teams. What it boils down to is that aircraft and the tricks played by the sky at night may not answer all the questions posed by those lights on the moors. There remains an element of mystery.

For the other stories my brother and I went to see John

Davies, the only inhabitant of a row of old, terraced cottages overlooking the railway and what used to be Crowden Station. He is an elderly, serene, quietly affable man who knows Crowden's history better than most because he has been part of it. And there is no nonsense about him. That day gave us sunshine, rain, mist, a hailstorm, and the sight of hills splashed with snow. John's cottage is isolated on the edge of the moors and as he opened the garden gate he told us: 'Had 40 sheep in t' garden during t' blizzard. They'd nowhere else to go.' Yes, a kind man too.

He said he would believe anything about Longdendale: 'It's a weird place at night.' There had always been rumours about ghosts and soldiers. As for the lights, he could not see those from where he lived but assumed they had something to do with aircraft. An aircraft was also the cause of one of three stories he could tell us. It was a Blenheim bomber that crashed on the moor.

They booked it as missing at sea. A hiker found it. There'd been snow and it had thawed. He saw what he thought was a white tent. Who'd be camping up here at this time of year? But there was a piece of body attached, and he got off as fast as he could. We went up Sunday. It was a nice day. The police, the RAF, gamekeepers, me and one or two more. There were about three in it. It was a terrible mess. Just exploded. It was hard lines, really: if he'd been a few feet higher he'd have missed it. But he didn't know where he was. Came from Church Fenton.

We fetched one or two things down as mementoes. Thick pieces of Perspex. I put them in t' garage down t' road. I was in there with a mate, working on motor bikes. It was a lovely moonlight night. Frosty. We had the Tilley lamp on. And there was like a cat's noise, but amplified a lot more. Snuffling around. I was amazed, not frightened. Immediately, it came to me – it's a big cat, a lion. What the 'eck's a lion doing around here? It sounds ridiculous. This lad said 'Don't go to t' door!' When I opened t' door there was nothing about. If there had been I'd have slammed t' door shut quick – but I don't think an asbestos hut would have been much good.

My father didn't believe in ghosts. But he told me 'There's only one thing I can say – I'd get rid of those bits o' Perspex if I were you.' So I took it right up t' moors and buried it.

John Davies worked in the signal box at Crowden and was among those often disturbed – day or night – by shouts of 'Nah!' (presumably a clipped version of the North's familiar exclamation 'Nah then!'). The plate-layer would go to the signal box and say 'What do you want?' and John would ask him what he meant. And either or both would investigate. They never found anyone.

His final story concerned a drive home from Glossop:

I got round Devil's Elbow, a mile the other side of Torside crossing, about level with the farm, and a great black wall appeared in front. I couldn't see through it. Had to stop right in front of it. It didn't frighten me but I had a queer sensation. It was like a massive black slug sliding across t' road and up to t' moor. It disappeared and I got out and had a look. But there was nothing there. I've been over there thousands of times and never seen anything like that before.

John told us this ten years after the incident. But within twenty-four hours of our meeting there was a newspaper report about a woman who was driving along a familiar road, the A21's Sevenoaks by-pass, when part of the way ahead was suddenly blocked by blackness . . .

A last note on gloomy Longdendale must concern the tunnel between Dunford Bridge and Woodhead. The first, single-track tunnel was constructed between 1838 and 1845 and at three miles and 66 yards was then the longest tunnel in the world. But it gave Woodhead a reputation as the rail-wayman's graveyard. The navvies (a far less fortunate breed than the navigators from whom the word was derived) worked in the most degrading conditions imaginable – and 33 were killed, 140 seriously hurt. When a second single-track tunnel was made, between 1847 and 1852, 28 men died during a cholera outbreak in 1849. A third tunnel, for electrified trains, was built from 1949 to 1954. Passengers use this route no longer. It is reserved for goods traffic. The civil engineer originally associated with the first tunnel, Charles Blacker Vignoles, had the unusual distinction of becoming a commissioned officer at the age of 18 months. His father died of wounds while fighting the French on Guadeloupe, in the Caribbean, and his mother lived only a week longer. The baby was taken prisoner by the French and in order to secure his release the commander of the English forces made Vignoles an ensign.

East of Woodhead the A628 passes Black Clough Bottom, a beautifully wooded glen, and then carves its way through desolate but impressively rugged country between Thurl-stone and Langsett Moors. During the stagecoach era there were two inns on this stretch. One was at Salter's Brook, so called because Cheshire salt was transported this way. There were many hill farms in the area in those pre-grouse days and the Saltersbrook Inn was popular with the shepherds. It was also popular with law-breakers because, like Three Shire Heads, it then marked the junction of three counties at a time when police forces had to stay on their own 'patches'. In the nineteenth century the gentry used to travel out to Salter's Brook to bet on prize fights and if the police turned up the 'ring' was quickly shifted into another county. In 1817 a second inn, the Plough and Harrow, was built farther east where the old and new roads diverge. A Woodhead fiddler was hired for opening day and the owners of the Saltersbrook Inn, resenting the competition, sarcastically nicknamed the new inn 'Fiddler's Green', a name that still applies to the same spot on the map. Known hereabouts as the Woodhead Pass, the A628 rises to 1,450ft before crossing the A616 at that renowned rendezvous for travellers, the Flouch Inn, which was obviously not designed to win beauty competitions.

West of Crowden is Lad's Leap, two rock ledges 43ft

apart. The Pennine Way goes up the deep, moorland valley of Crowden Great Brook past the chutes and falls of Oaken Clough; past Laddow Rocks (where the climbers have almost exclusively Mancunian accents); and past the outcrops known as Crowden Castles and Red Ratcher. So to Black Hill and masses of oozing peat. As you mucky your boots and addle your brains trying to sort out these 'undefined' stretches of the Pennine Way, you realise that the cartographers are telling you politely: 'Sorry, mate. Can't help.' The 1,908ft summit of Black Hill is called Soldier's Lump because of its use for military surveys.

West of Laddow Rocks is Chew Reservoir, at 1,600ft the highest in the Peak District. Down Chew Brook is a large, square boulder known as the Sugar Lump and – just south of the A635 – Dove Stone Reservoir and the ruins of Ashway Gap House. This was built in 1850 as a hunting lodge and served as a hospital in the First World War and a prisoner-of-war camp in the Second. One of the rooms is supposed to be haunted by the ghost of the original owner's brother, James Platt, who died in it after a shooting accident, recorded by a memorial cross on the moors.

Ramblers between the wars were often grateful to reach either (or both) of two oddly named inns on the A635. These were Bill's o' Jack's, near the reservoirs on the moors above Greenfield, and the Isle of Skye, nearer Holmfirth. Both were closed long ago. In 1832 the former attracted notoriety and thousands of visitors after the murder of the eponymous publican, William Bradbury, and his son Thomas ('Tom o' Bill's'). It was in this same area of Saddleworth Moor that a child's body was found at Hollin Brown Knoll during investigations into the Moors Murders. The urban district of Saddleworth once covered 18,000 acres and about 50 per cent of it was over 1,000ft. Villages and hamlets were thinly scattered along valleys cut into wild moorland and much of the scenery remains unchanged. But the textile industry – plus a canal, a railway, and improved roads – transformed the character of the Tame Valley. At Standedge the canal between Ashton-under-Lyne and Huddersfield had a section on which bargees propelled boats through a tunnel by 'legging', as in the Speedwell Mine at Castleton.

The bleak heights of Standedge overlook Marsden, which lies in a dale watered by a stream that descends from Wessenden Moor, filling reservoirs on the way. One of Marsden's eighteenth-century residents was the mother of General James Wolfe, though he was born while she was visiting Westerham in Kent. During the Luddite riots William Horsfall, a Marsden mill-owner who had introduced machinery, was murdered while on his way home from Huddersfield market. Samuel Laycock, the Ebenezer Elliott of the western Pennines, was born at Marsden in 1826 and worked at Horsfall's mill. He wrote dialect stories and songs about factory life and his direct, homespun style earned him great popularity among the kind of people he was writing about. It was in Laycock's time that the mountain hare was introduced in the Marsden area, for hunting purposes. Meltham, now a small textile town, appeared in the Domesday Book and is probably much older, because there was an Iron Age farm near by. Meltham Moor has a renowned rocking stone. In June, sheepdog trials are held on Harden Moss.

A television series, 'The Last of the Summer Wine', has made most of us familiar with the environs of Holmfirth, where tall houses are perched on steep hillsides in the valley of the River Holme. There is hardly enough level ground to accommodate a football pitch. Holmfirth has other claims to our attention in its pork pies and a pub called 'The Post Card', which has a sign representing a post card complete with dated stamp. An unusual memorial near the church is a little pillar erected to mark the peace treaty signed by Britain and France at Amiens in 1802. On this pillar – and on the wall of a butcher's shop across the river – are marks indicating the height the water reached during a terrible flood in February 1852. After days of heavy rain the embankment of

Bilberry Reservoir was undermined by springs and collapsed. In half an hour the reservoir was empty. Almost 90 million gallons of water poured into the Holme Valley and through the town, smashing houses, mills, bridges and trees. In addition to the eighty-one dead, many people were homeless and about 7,000 were put out of work.

An interesting old building in Holme, up the valley to the south-west, is a Sunday School with a house attached. Quaintly surmounted by a bell in a sturdy stone housing, this structure stands in the angle formed by two roads. Carved into the appropriate walls are hands with fingers pointing to Holmfirth and Woodhead respectively. Holme Moss and Heyden Moor are popular areas for local outings and the spectacular drive down to Woodhead exposes the authentic character of the Peak District's northern moorlands, contrasting sharply with the fields and woodlands of the gentler country to the north-east. Holme Moss television station, opened in 1951, has a slim 750ft tower that disappears into the clouds and has become a famous landmark on the most dramatic approach to the Peak District.

East of the Holmfirth–Woodhead road is Grains Moss, the source of the River Don, which flows through Penistone and Stocksbridge down to Sheffield. We should note the proximity of Denby Dale, renowned for its annual production of a giant pie. The first of these was baked in 1788 to celebrate George III's recovery from his first serious mental illness. The 1964 pie honoured six royal births and weighed over six tons. For centuries Penistone's markets and fairs made it one of the most important agricultural centres in the Peak District. What is less well known is that the many Wordsworths assembled in the graveyard since the fourteenth century were the poet's ancestors. It was in this churchyard that a boy blinded by smallpox taught himself to read by running his fingers over the inscriptions. He was Nicholas Saunderson, born at nearby Thurlstone in 1682, who was to become a distinguished mathematician and a competent flautist.

Three miles to the south-west is the isolated, pre-Norman hamlet of Upper Midhope. Its neighbour Midhopestones, mostly built round a steep and winding lane, has two unusual buildings. By the junction of the Penistone road and the A616 is an incongruous four-storey structure that looks like an unsuccessful compromise between house and factory. It was in fact the Rose and Crown, which rose from the ground early in the nineteenth century but never made the grade as a coaching inn. Midhopestones also has a charming little church by a bend in that hillside lane. It dates from 1705, has a gallery, and is largely home-grown. The box pews were made from local oak and the glass came from three miles away at Bolsterstone, an old manorial village that somehow produced a male voice choir good enough to teach the Welsh a thing or two by winning the 1972 Eisteddfod. One of our Hathersage acquaintances, Joseph Sheldon, was buried at Bolsterstone. He worked for Samuel Fox at Stocksbridge, which could be described as an outcrop of industrial Sheffield. The Wharncliffe area – the Chase, the Rocks, the Wood – used to be hunting country and a fashionable beauty spot until improved communications made the Peak District easier to reach. Wharncliffe Side had a thriving smithy. Much of the old charm is still there if you look for it.

You will have noticed that, in the cause of tidiness and to avoid zigzagging about, we have been skirting around a substantial chunk of the Peak District. Let us now make it the last act in our little drama.

Two miles east of the Snake Inn, flowing down to the Woodlands Valley, there is a deep cleft in the southern flank of Bleaklow. This is the remote, unspoilt, magically secluded Alport Dale, where you can dream your dreams and step back in time. It has two remarkable features – one natural, the other a piece of social history. The Tower and Alport Castles, the cliff from which The Tower slowly detached itself, constitute one of Britain's largest, most spectacularly mind-boggling landslips. If you want to find out about the erosive possibilities of combining gritstone and shale, this is the place (though Mam Tor is a substantial appetiser). They say that at times the erosion can be seen and heard. From a distance The Tower, now isolated, looks like the crumbled ruins of a man-made fortress – an impression enhanced by the boulder-strewn depressions around it. The visual effect of this geological joke is weird. Haunting.

The unworldly privacy of Alport Dale made it the perfect refuge for persecuted non-conformists towards the end of the seventeenth century. They could meet there and do their own thing without risk of detection. Thus was born a tradition that developed into an annual Methodist 'love feast', a sacramental ceremony held in a barn at Alport Castles Farm, usually on the first Sunday in July. The ceremony has not changed much. Nor has the barn.

Three miles north of Alport Dale is Swains Greave, a boggy bowl known locally as the 'Skimming Dish'. This formerly wooded hollow is the source of the Peak District's longest and most important river, the Derwent, which flows almost the entire length of the national park and covers a total of sixty miles before joining the Trent. For three miles it makes a dodging, tumbling escape from Bleaklow and Howden Moors to Slippery Stones. Local folk used to gather watercress here until the supply was discovered and ravaged by navvies working on the Langsett, Midhope, Howden and Derwent reservoirs. From the Flouch Inn near Langsett there is a ruggedly exhilarating walk to Slippery Stones across a high, wild landscape along an ancient track that used to be called Cartgate but is now Cut Gate. In September 1959, about 200 people gathered at Slippery Stones on the Derby-shire–Yorkshire boundary for the formal reopening of a packhorse bridge that had taken twenty years to travel five miles. It used to stand near the gates to Derwent Hall and in 1938, before the village was pulled down to make way for Ladybower Reservoir, there was a public appeal for funds so that the bridge could be dismantled and the stones marked in readiness for re-erection elsewhere. But what with the war, doubts about a suitable site, and the cost of re-erection, the seventeenth-century bridge remained in storage at what used to be Abbey Grange – east of the present Derwent Reservoir – until 1959. Only the flagstones could not be saved when the bridge was taken down. Those installed at Slippery Stones came from demolished houses in Sheffield.

Slippery Stones is the northern extremity of Derwent Dale, which extends as far as the A57 and consists almost entirely of three reservoirs. The Derwent Valley Water Board did the job in three stages. The Howden and Derwent reservoirs were constructed between 1901 and 1911. From 1921 to 1930 water from the Ashop and Alport was diverted into the Derwent Reservoir by driving a tunnel 1,000 yards long through the intervening hill. The final stage, the Ladybower Reservoir, took from 1935 to 1939. The water goes to Leicester, Sheffield, Derby, and Nottingham by means of underground aqueducts, superficially identified by stone inspection chambers.

Conifer forests were planted alongside the reservoirs. So the basic blue and green of Derwent Dale's present scenery has to a great extent been artificially contrived. It looks none the worse for that except for the formality with which such natural components as trees and water have been arranged and the chilling, massively grey walls of the dams in an otherwise colourful dale. The high backdrop of moorland softens what might otherwise be the hard lines of a regimented topography. This is the Goyt Valley all over again, but on a larger scale. Man has taken water from the wilderness and destroyed two villages and a peaceful farming community with its roots in the Middle Ages. In return he has richly enhanced the dramatic content of the view. These lakes are beautiful memorials to a terrible destruction.

A temporary village called Birchinlee but popularly known as 'Tin Town' was erected to accommodate the work force needed to build the first two reservoirs. Now a plantation, the site was on the north-western flank of what became Derwent Reservoir. There were about 400 workers and including families this self-contained village had about 1,000 inhabitants – and its own shops, canteen, school, mission, hospital, doss-house and recreation room (even its own football team). The people lived in dog-legged rows of identical single-storey huts made of corrugated iron and lined with wood. An old photograph shows the place swarming with booted children, the boys in knickerbockers, the girls in smocks and puffed sleeves and high collars. A special Bamford–Howden railway, demanding the construction of an ugly wooden viaduct at Ashopton, carried stone and other materials to the dams and was also used by Birchinlee families on day outings. Bamford doubtless found them more congenial than the dreaded eighteenth-century savages who came down from the Derwent woodlands to raid the village and abduct any women they fancied.

Those first two reservoirs had a high cost in men killed or mutilated by explosions or other accidents. But the job was done – and in 1914 Birchinlee and the railway were taken apart and wiped off the landscape. Some of the discarded track was taken to France and used for transporting troops. Early in 1943 Derwent Reservoir (plus a few others scattered around Langsett and Bradfield) served a more startling wartime purpose. The 'Dam Busters' (the new 617 Squadron) used it for low-level night flights over water in preparation for their assault on the Möhne and Eder dams in the Ruhr valley. That training was hazardous and it could have been over Derwent that Guy Gibson's bomb-aimer, Spam Spafford, closely confronted by the waters of a reservoir while peering through the Lancaster's nose, relieved a tense silence with a heartfelt: 'Christ, this is bloody dangerous!' Gibson's black, beer-drinking Labrador, Nigger, was on that training flight – dozing . . . Much of the 1955 film *The Dam Busters* was made at Derwent Reservoir and in 1977 five survivors of the raid went back to Derwent to celebrate the thirty-fourth anniversary by watching the last operational Lancaster 'buzz' the dam.

That reference to Nigger reminds me that shepherds had a tough life on the often hostile moors around Derwent Dale. West of Derwent Reservoir is an isolated peak known as Lost Lad. One spring a shepherd was attracted to the spot by the words 'Lost Lad' scratched on a rock, and found the body of a shepherd boy who had missed his way while gathering sheep in bad weather during the winter. Just north of Derwent dam, beside the road, is a memorial slab facing across Howden Reservoir to the distant moors. It reads:

'In commemoration of the devotion of Tip, the sheepdog which stayed by the body of her dead master, Mr Joseph Tagg, on the Howden Moors for fifteen weeks from 12th December 1953 to 27th March 1954. Erected by public subscription.'

Tip presumably survived by nibbling nature's emergency rations: small animals or birds weakened, perhaps frozen to death, in the course of a severe winter. Tagg, 86, was a sheep farmer renowned for his prize-winning dogs. He was living in semi-retirement at Yorkshire Bridge but on the day of his disappearance paid a nostalgic visit to the site of his childhood home, Ronksley Farm, at the bottom of Linch Clough. His body was found on the western side of Grinah Grain (Ridgewalk Moor) with Tip lying a few yards away. The 11-year-old bitch was thin, feeble, and bedraggled and had to be carried part of the way home – but was then nursed back to health and enjoyed celebrity status until she died almost a year later. A northern folk song on this theme contains the line: 'Whilst owt were left o' Will 'e'd stop an' mind it'.

Those first two reservoirs were made so long ago that it is doubtful if anyone can remember, first hand, the peaceful piece of England they destroyed and drowned. The Ladybower Reservoir is a different story. Filling did not begin until 1943. Since then it has swallowed two villages, thirteen farms, and about five miles of well-remembered roads. Ladybower covers 504 acres of memories. Its perimeter is thirteen miles. It extends for more than three miles of the Derwent and two miles of the Woodlands (Ashop) Valley. Two viaducts were needed to carry more than five miles of new roads. Can you imagine how it feels, now, to have lived under those still waters, or merely to remember honeyed weekends among those gently wooded lanes, flowered fields and sturdy houses and farms that looked as if nothing could ever budge them?

All that was yesterday. Gone, except for the pictures in the album and in the mind's eye. Yet I recently drove down to Ladybower late on an autumn day in the first shadowy promise of dusk. The bright, low sun was having its last fling and playing marvellous tricks with the lighting. And the colours of Ladybower and its trees and moors were so radiantly lovely that the sight of them caught the breath. As I said, a beautiful memorial to a terrible destruction.

There was no 'Tin Town' this time. All unskilled labour was recruited through Sheffield Labour Exchange and the Water Board hired coaches to carry the workmen to and fro.

Just below Derwent dam (an awesome thing when water is thunderously cascading down its face) a lane crosses the dale and then runs south to the bottom of Mill Brook, where the village of Derwent used to stand. It was not a picture-postcard scene in the Ashopton class, but when viewed from the west against the background of Derwent Edge and Back Tor it had a special charm. The original settlement was really an offshoot of Abbey Grange (a mile or so north), which was founded in the reign of Richard I. The monks built four chapels, two bridges across the Derwent, and a mill. It is said that during one of the Scottish invasions, in 1648 or 1745, Scottish soldiers were imprisoned in the Abbey's own chapel and starved to death. Derwent Hall was built in 1672. In 1886 the Duke of Norfolk bought the place and enlarged it, adding a private chapel. The Hall looked pleasantly solid, with creeper-clad walls and a country garden. In 1932 it became a youth hostel.

Derwent Hall, the packhorse bridge, the little church, a few cottages and a school were the heart of the village. All were demolished in 1943 except for the church tower, which refused to die. It rose defiantly above the rising water and, after submersion, reappeared during the droughts of 1948 and 1959 – and people walked out to it across the bed of the reservoir and looked around and remembered. It is difficult to describe the extent to which that tower and all it represented captured the hearts and imaginations of those who knew and cared about Derwent. But the desperate sadness of its isolation was a heart-aching spectacle: and also a hazardous temptation. So it was finally demolished – architectural euthanasia.

Derwent's dead were exhumed in 1940 and reinterred at Bamford. At the bottom of the hill below Derwent church-yard was a war memorial. This was moved and re-erected beside the road about a mile up Derwent Dale, where it faces straight across the reservoir towards the vanished village that the men named on the memorial used to know.

Between Derwent and Ashopton the river was narrow, rocky and attractively shaded. Ashopton stood near the confluence of the Ashop and Derwent and what remains of it lies under the water at the Sheffield end of the main viaduct. While Ashopton was still intact, that mighty viaduct was already towering over it like a symbol of doom. Ashopton, formerly Cocksbridge, consisted of an inn that looked more like a solid and rather staid private house, a Methodist chapel, the Toll Bar House, two farms, six cottages and a bridge. There was not much to the place, but it was a well-known beauty spot on the Sheffield–Glossop road and looked sturdy enough to have centuries of living left in it. Pendulous branches overhung a steep, wooded lane, a delightful spot when the sun was shining through. There were trees, too, by a river that laughed its way round boulders. And grassy banks and hedgerows and splashes of woodland in the background. That was all. But there was a poetry in Ashopton. The quiet kind.

In spite of its watery continuity there is a sharp contrast between the two ends of Derwent Dale. The rugged moors of the north are for sheep and grouse, mountain hares and bog-trotters. The Ashopton end is busy with traffic yet impressively dominated by the heights on either side. Crook Hill, rising between the two arms of Ladybower Reservoir, has a farm that has been there since the fifteenth century – plus a superb ridge walk to Lockerbrook Heights. Frankly, though, it is difficult to give any scenic walk in the Peak District pride of place over that along Derwent Edge on the eastern side of the valley. It can be approached via the Ladybower Inn (a former sheep farm converted to profit from coach traffic when the Sheffield–Glossop road was opened in 1821) and Cutthroat Bridge, which also dates from about 1820–21. This interesting name may be derived from the fact that in the sixteenth century a man was found with his throat cut near an older bridge a little farther upstream.

Derwent Edge has a majestic outline and the track along the top commands a panorama remarkable in its range and beauty. There are reservoirs below, heaving moorland in every direction, and great sweeps of woodland and bracken, heather and bilberry. And right beside us, all the time, are crazy gritstone outcrops. The Hurkling Stones is a common label for isolated rocks that seem to be bending or crouching. The Coach and Horses, known to map-makers as the Wheel Stones, are an extraordinary sight when dramatically silhouetted on the skyline. There really does seem to be a stage-coach racing along the horizon. After that come the Salt Cellar, Dovestone Tor, the Cakes of Bread, and the 1,765ft Back Tor, all of which have something special to offer in the way of visual entertainment. A further point in favour of Derwent Edge is that it tends to be relatively uncluttered with the kind of trippers who flow along fashionably grooved channels. Perhaps it is too close to Sheffield and too far from Manchester to attract either army in full force. Whatever the reason, the human traffic is seldom irksome.

Between the Cakes of Bread and Back Tor a track branches off towards plantations and reservoirs a mile or so to the east. This brings us to a lane just north of the Strines Inn, a familiar landmark in a lonely setting. ('Strines' is old English for 'watercourses'.) From the north, the lane rises sharply towards the inn and at the top of this climb, on the left by a telegraph pole, is a roadside stone bearing the words 'Take Off'. The story behind this puzzling imperative is that in the old days 'chain' horses were kept handy to help wagons up such steep ascents – rather like hooking an extra locomotive onto a train in need of more power. The 'Take Off' sign was the formal equivalent of 'You're on your own from here, chum.' Incidentally, Charlotte Brontë (and Jane Eyre, of course) may have stepped off the coach a mile or so south of the Strines Inn.

The winding lane running north-east towards Bradfield takes us into a suddenly gentler and more intimate kind of scenery, much more than four miles from Derwent Dale in terms of character. True, there are more reservoirs. But essentially this is a green, pastoral land of pleasantly wooded valleys and hills that merge with the moors without being dominated by them. On a prominent height south of Strines Reservoir is a tower known as Boot's Folly, built for a Sheffield man called Charles Boot. He was impressed by a similar tower constructed on Ughill Moors for the Duke of Norfolk's gamekeeper, and devised an imitation for his own use. In the middle of the nineteenth century the Duke of Norfolk engaged able-bodied paupers to work in groups of ten clearing a large expanse of land between Ughill Moors and the A57. Now called Hollow Meadows, it formerly had the jocular title of 'New England'.

The story of the Bilberry Reservoir at Holmfirth had an appalling parallel at Bradfield in 1864. It was the worst disaster of its kind in Britain's history: the Sheffield Flood. The Dale Dike Reservoir had gradually been filling up. At midnight on 11 March there was a landslip and the newly built dam burst. About 700 million gallons of water rushed down the Loxley Valley through Low Bradfield, Loxley, Malin Bridge, and Sheffield, uprooting trees and destroying houses, mills, bridges, and everything else in its path. A Bradfield miller looked out of his window and saw his mill swept away. The dead numbered 244, including an entire family of ten, and almost 20,000 people became homeless. The devastation scarred Loxley for many years. In 1940 Barnes Wallis, already working on the 'bouncing' bomb that was to be used in the raid on the Möhne and Eder dams, went to Sheffield to discuss the bomb casings with steel experts. On that same trip the details of the Sheffield Flood told him all he wanted to know about the effect the bombs might have.

The quaintly named Haychatter Inn lies west of Low Bradfield, a neat old village convenient for excursionists from north-western Sheffield. Low Bradfield has some three-storey houses that go back to the days when framework knitting was a cottage industry. It used to have a 'hiring' fair, too. High Bradfield, which stands on a ledge above the valley, has a roomy church built to serve a large though thinly populated parish. Its striking situation commands wide views. At the churchyard gate is an oddly designed two-up and two-down 'watch house' built in 1745 for a guard who was employed to frustrate body-snatchers. Founded in the twelfth century, the church has a Celtic cross that probably dates from the tenth. The pulpit has handsome carvings of Christ and the Evangelists. Another unusual feature is the huge parish chest which, except for the lid, was made from a single block of oak in 1615. It contained documents and accounts and had four locks. The strangest thing about the church is a tiny, sunken room near the altar. Complete with fireplace, this former dungeon was used for the overnight accommodation of visiting priests from Ecclesfield Priory, north of Sheffield, and later became a vestry. It looks like an elfin squash court.

On either side of High Bradfield there is evidence of ancient fortifications. Bailey Hill, with its ditch and mound, was presumably surmounted by a palisade in the days when this remote and unruly region was vulnerable to attack. Saxons may have used it as an assembly area, but the defensive works were probably Norman. Castle Hill has less obvious vestiges of what may have been a fortified observation point.

Broomhead Hall, to the north-west, was severely damaged in 1642 when occupied by a Parliamentary army after a six-week siege. Near by are two puzzling defensive earth-works: puzzling because, like the Grey Ditch at Bradwell, they cannot be dated. Bar Dyke is about 350 yards long. And overlooking Ewden Beck is a rampart stretching for half a mile. Well, there is a legend about a battle between Mercia and Northumbria on the desolate, windswept heights of Broomhead Moor. We shall never get at the truth. But the Peak District would not be half as much fun without its mysteries.

See you on the tops. And look out for Roman soldiers.

Bibliography

It would be impossible to recall, and impracticable to list, everything the author has read about the Peak District since he first knew it as a child. The publications listed here are merely those he happened to find most useful as occasional consultants during the preparation of this book. It should not be assumed that this is a comprehensive guide to other works on the subject, or even a selection of the best.

Mary Andrews: *Long Ago in Peakland.*

F. R. Banks: *The Peak District.*

Roy Christian: *The Peak District.*

John Derry: *Across the Derbyshire Moors* (revised by G. H. B. Ward).

The Dictionary of National Biography.

K. C. Edwards: *The Peak District.*

Trevor D. Ford and J. H. Rieuwerts (editors): *Lead Mining in the Peak District.*

Antonia Fraser: *Mary Queen of Scots.*

R. A. Frost and P. Shooter: *Birds of the Peak District.*

Arthur Mee: *Cheshire*; *Derbyshire* (revised and edited by F. R. Banks); and *Yorkshire West Riding.*

Sheffield Clarion Ramblers (various handbooks).

Roland Smith: *First and Last.*

Henry Thorold: *Staffordshire* (a Shell Guide).

Ethel Carleton Williams: *Companion into Derbyshire.*

Acknowledgements

The content of *The Peak District Companion* is based on forty years of personal acquaintance with its fells, dales, and villages, its history and customs. This background knowledge was amplified by a study of a wide variety of other publications on the subject and updated by more than a year's thorough research, on the spot, in the entire area covered by the book. In all this the author was encouraged and assisted by relatives and friends who share his enthusiasm, and by many others who kindly helped to verify, expand and in some cases correct the information assembled.

The author is particularly grateful to several ministers of religion, the editors of church and national-park pamphlets, the staff of Sheffield City Libraries, Peter Bell of the Riber Castle wildlife reserve, Michael Pearman of the Chatsworth Library, Derbyshire Countryside Ltd., the librarians of Sheffield Newspapers and the *Derby Evening Telegraph*, and David Tomlinson of *Country Life*.

Thanks to these and a host of others who contributed their time, their expertise, or merely their support and opinions, *The Peak District Companion* is more comprehensive, more accurate, and more interesting than it might have been. The author is therefore very grateful indeed for all the help so willingly given.

Index

INDEX

INDEX